deconstructing the dish

deconstru

inspirations for modern-day cuisine

cting the dish

David Adjey

foreword by Dan Aykroyd

whitecap

Edited by Lesley Cameron
Proofread by Taryn Boyd
Design by Stacey Noyes / LuzForm Design
Food Photography by Christopher Wadsworth

Printed in Canada

Library and Archives Canada Cataloguing in Publication

Adjey, David, 1964-
Deconstructing the dish : inspirations for modern-day cuisine / David Adjey.

Includes index.
ISBN 978-1-55285-897-4
ISBN 1-55285-897-9

1. Cookery. I. Title.
TX714.A454 2007 641.5 C2007-901706-1

The publisher acknowledges the financial support of the Government of Canada through the Book Publishing Industry Development Program (BPIDP) and the province of British Columbia through the Book Publishing Tax Credit.

To Carmen, my partner in life and in business

I couldn't do it without you.

Contents

Foreword

A frosty Ontario night pressed in against my log cabin windows when David Adjey first brought forth his New Year's Feast. Commissioned by my wife, Donna, on a one-time trial basis, Mr. Adjey agreed to man our eight-burner Viking stove with the hope of preparing Donna's menu to the standard set by a US Southern Beauty's knowledge of comfort cooking. Maple syrup-glazed ham sandwiches on fluffy, white roadhouse biscuits with grape jelly, mustard and bib lettuce inside; pears and pitted cherry meat au jus; rosemary-roasted turkey with pearl onions, elephant garlic buds and sliced pan-browned homestyle russet potatoes all in a brothy roux; Porterhouse steaks sliced Chateaubriand-style in their juices with creamed horseradish, Yorkshire pudding and green peas; raisin and rum sea scallops browned in a pan by Adjey like a gunslinger as he was pulling off the chopped bok choy, green beans and banana peppers cooked in a wok for our spicy vegetarian eldest daughter.

It was evident to us all within less than two hours that we were in the presence of a culinary genius with an appropriate commando approach to the hot-delivered, speed-cooking required in our house. The wines, the finishes, the desserts—a case of Billecart-Salmon rosé champagne, a buttery Puligny Montrachet, Château Latour 1990, Mocha Dacquoise, chocolate devil's food cake, coffees with Patron XØ and Frangelico followed by good smokes. This was a night of gastronomic ecstasy that will be sumptuously rolled over in our salivary memories until the end of time.

From that evening on it was a joy to have David stay in a single-wide trailer by the lake on special occasions. The outdoors touched his soul. Summer came, and with it came his grill skills—lime-infused lobster and shrimp, tiny bite-sized mustard lamb chops, marinated chicken wings and legs, Florentine thinly cut spadas and steaks with the simplest finger touches of oil and slivered garlic Good Fellas-style.

When word spread of the Left Bank Experience (David's platform on Queen Street West in Toronto) it wasn't long before five-star resorts in the US began to call. Santa Barbara's world-famous San Ysidro Ranch was the beneficiary of David's talent and a happy life ensued until, like many Canadian ex-patriots, he felt the urge to return home. The powerhouse known as Nectar resulted. Some day in our dreams the Aykroyds hope that David Adjey, or any one of his designates, might happen to confront our Viking stove again. If so, he, she or they may be assured that their accommodations at our place will definitely be upgraded from the single-wide trailer to the Keith Richards Memorial bedroom in my writing tower.

Meanwhile, we now have this magnificent book to see us through.

Dan Aykroyd
at Oak Roads Farm, Bearshead Cabin

Preface

As a professional I'm always challenged by the disparity between what I want to cook and what my customers want to eat. However, I learned long ago from some of my great mentors that if you cook from the heart, you're cooking with passion ... and everyone will enjoy the meal.

Funny how when you're asked to write a cookbook, for most chefs, it's about writing a book for yourself, a chance to really showcase your culinary accomplishments.

But after diving into the creation of this book, rolling up my sleeves and cooking in my home, there was the realization that cookbooks have to be easily understood to be an easy and useful tool for your kitchen.

We struggle as chefs and authors to categorize or subdivide our thoughts in the way that we cook. Many won't admit that we eat through our emotions. Hence my idea to divide this book to reflect my approach to cooking as influenced by external factors: When I'm Cool, When I'm Cold, When I'm Warm, When I'm Hot.

So, *Deconstructing the Dish* is how I look at ingredients for my main meal. It's how I cook for myself.

A cookbook should not be a word-for-word regurgitation of a chef's dish but rather a mad scientist's periodic table with a formula to create, and guidance on what ingredients and combinations are successful.

I hope that many years from now this book, tattered and dogeared, is an essential tool in your kitchen, containing all your personal notes, reminders, additions and changes ... it's your cookbook now. Use it to its fullest potential. It's okay to change a recipe and make it yours. Don't be afraid to make your own notes on the pages. Find what works for you, and mark it down for all time.

Only then will I truly feel accomplished; that I've passed something forward. Experience passion for food. Embrace the challenge of creation.

Acknowledgments

To every sous chef, line cook and dishwasher that I've slugged it out with over the years. I truly couldn't have done it without you.

To my publisher, Robert, for believing in me and my food. In the midst of restaurant openings, a TV show and writing the book, I'd like to say I owe you more than dinner for your patience and support. To the soldiers at Whitecap, thank you so much for making the hardest project in my life that much easier.

To every supplier whom I've woken up in the middle of the night and all the delivery men who have pushed their trucks through extreme weather to get my product in the kitchen, thank you so much for your dedication to the industry.

To every storekeeper whose path I've crossed from Latin, Asian and open city markets, you've contributed to a constant learning experience with new ingredients and you all took the time to explain the ingredient and how to best use it.

To Jameel and Andrea at Tricon for giving me the opportunity to share my passion for food on "Restaurant Makeover," my sincere thank you.

To my fellow chefs, too many to name, it's our mutual respect for one another that makes me proud to be a member of this club. Mondays will always be our Fridays.

To Jamie, Ryan and Peter. Remember, one chef in the family is enough.

To my mom and dad, I look back on your gourmet club dinners of the 70s as the catalyst behind my passion for cooking. Thank you from my heart. I love you both.

Introduction

My aim when cooking is not only to see the big picture, but also to focus on the most minute detail of a dish. I'm told by friends, staff and fellow chefs that the way I talk, my enthusiasm for new ideas in the kitchen, the way I use my hands (who knew?!) when explaining the flavor all give a true tactile response to a listener even before the dish is presented to them. Those who have been at one of my restaurants and have seen the creative chaos for themselves (and, I have to confess, heard the occasional swearing!) tell me they have experienced true passion for food. I try to define cuisine so that it has a sensory translation—I want dishes to have a taste and a smell as they are described.

I love to observe the way things are put together in all aspects of life. For me things are products of smaller things: a good painting is a collection of well-placed pigments, a car is just a list of parts ingeniously crafted to work together. And so a dish is more than just a grouping of food for me; it is a series of elements, of taste, color, texture and aroma.

By looking at each dish as a sum of its parts, I have tried to simplify the complex and make sense of the many layers that make up a single dish. The challenge is to break things down to their smallest units to be able to restructure or understand them as a whole through their individuality. This allows me to produce very simple-to-follow ideas and descriptions, even when concluding very complex finales.

Deconstructing the Dish starts at the finish line. I dissect and explain each dish as comprised of building blocks, each hidden within the finished dish. Exploring the building blocks of fine dishes will give the reader an understanding of how to approach dishes by starting from the center (the principle) and working out to the garnish, the vegetable, the sauce, etc. This basic new understanding will empower the reader to use all, or some, of the parts in a modular way, combining building blocks from one dish with building blocks from another, adding their own parts to an already existing equation. Learning about the elements of a dish and how to place them together, combined with a whole bunch of wonderful elemental recipes, will inspire the reader to create dishes of their very own.

I do not intend *Deconstructing the Dish* to be a conventional recipe book by which people may memorize or copy recipe after recipe; it is instead intended to be a source of inspiration, providing a mythology on how to attach the creation of a plate. Simply, *Deconstructing the Dish* provides people with some of the pieces required to get the motor of imagination running. Then, cook with passion!

David Adjey

David's 12 Rules

Chefs, not owners, write menus.

Stay true to your vision.

Always taste first before your guests taste for you.

Never do it for the money.

Invest fully in the whole culture of cooking, from tools to travel to reading.

Try something weird on a menu, once.

Cook from a different region in the world at least once a week.

Never replace butter with anything except butter.

Veal jus just makes everything tastes better.

Respect the storage of spices—think cigars and humidors.

Talk to chefs. Ask them what you don't already know.

Never order off a menu that's bigger than your underwear.

Cool

September | October | November

When I'm Cool

September | October | November

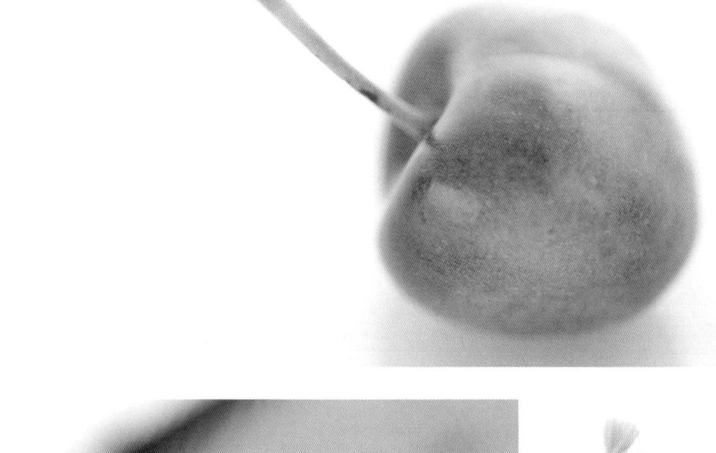

It's all about getting the most from the last push of summer's best bounty. Or at least, that's in my mind! We are bombarded with special events to cook for at this time of year: Labor Day, Thanksgiving and the harvest and wine festivals keep a chef on his toes. Whether I'm cooking for a wine festival in the Okanagan or a private dinner in Toronto, there's an energy in the air during the fall that is contagious. If you're a real food fan, you'll know what I mean.

For my customers and their special evening, I'm always looking for that "lottery ticket" ingredient that they haven't experienced to its fullest potential. I'm looking for the best quality, best ripeness, best color and, of course, the "wow" factor when they see the finished plate. For example, if you ever find yourself in the Eastern Townships, outside of Montreal, just ask anyone you see for the best-tasting duck in the world. You will find yourself on the door steps of Elise François—duck farmer of Aux Champs d'Elise. I think he's 90 years old. You can't miss him.

Dom Rebel
EST. MTL
BORN IN 1982

veal rib eye

shoestring potatoes | haricots verts | bovine vinaigrette

My advice when buying veal is to chat with your butcher about who produces the veal available in your area. There are numerous suppliers of free-range veal, and they are your best option both for flavor and to salve your conscience. Veal jus, or black gold as we call it in the restaurant world, is a huge ordeal to make, but when you do make it, freeze some for a dish like this. Fast and big-time flavor.

To build the dish
veal rib eye
veal rub
shoestring potatoes
fry dust
haricots verts
spiced pecans
bovine vinaigrette

Serves 4

For the veal rib eye

2 lb (1 kg) veal rib eye, center cut
1 Tbsp (15 mL) olive oil
1 tsp (5 mL) coarse salt
1 tsp (5 mL) freshly ground black pepper
2 Tbsp (30 mL) veal rub

Preheat oven to 350°F (160°C). Place a wire rack over a sheet pan.

Rub the rib eye with the olive oil and season with salt and pepper. In a large sauté pan over high heat, sear the rib eye on all sides until golden brown, about 2–3 minutes per side. Remove and rest, tented with aluminum foil, on a wooden cutting board until cool enough to touch.

Using your hands, massage the veal rub all over the rib eye until evenly distributed. Transfer to the prepared sheet pan and roast on the middle rack of the oven for 15 minutes. Remove from the oven and rest, tented with aluminum foil again, in a warm place for 5 minutes.

For the veal rub

½ cup (125 mL) scallions
1 tsp (5 mL) thyme leaves
½ cup (125 mL) flat-leaf parsley leaves
6 cloves garlic, peeled
1 lemon, zest only
½ cup (125 mL) grape seed oil

In a food processor fitted with a metal blade, process the scallions, thyme, parsley, garlic and zest into a smooth paste. Scrape down the sides of the bowl once. Add the grape seed oil slowly through the feed tube while the machine is running. Transfer to a clean nonreactive bowl, cover and refrigerate until needed.

For the shoestring potatoes

3 extra-large russet potatoes
2 Tbsp (30 mL) rice wine vinegar
1 tsp (5 mL) fry dust
vegetable oil for frying

Preheat deep-fryer to 375°F (190°C).

Wash the potatoes under cold running water to remove any soil. Over a bowl filled with cold water and the 2 Tbsp (30 mL) of rice wine vinegar, carefully cut the potatoes into long strips on the medium blade of a Japanese mandoline. Wash the potatoes again until the water runs clear. Transfer to a salad spinner to remove as much moisture as possible. Remove and add to the deep-fryer in small batches. Cook until golden brown, about 3–4 minutes. Remove from the fryer, season with fry dust and transfer to a paper towel-lined bowl. Keep them warm as you continue to fry the remaining potatoes.

For the fry dust

1 Tbsp (15 mL) coarse salt
1 Tbsp (15 mL) ground celery seeds
1 Tbsp (15 mL) ground coriander seeds
1 tsp (5 mL) smoked paprika
½ tsp (2 mL) ground chili flakes

In a large nonreactive bowl mix all the fry dust ingredients until incorporated. Transfer to an airtight container and store at room temperature for up to 1 month.

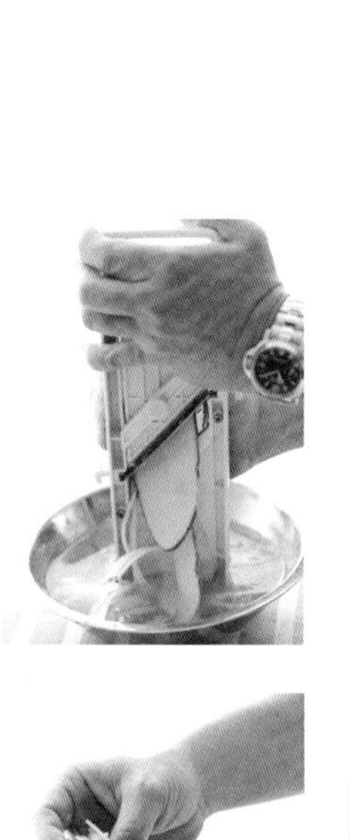

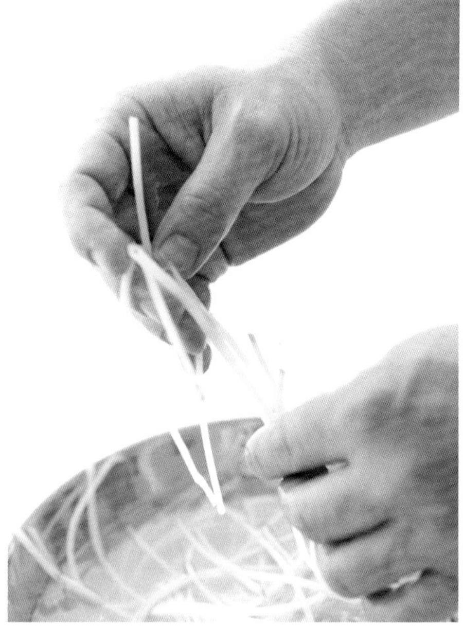

veal rib eye (continued)

For the haricots verts

2 Tbsp (30 mL) coarse salt
½ lb (250 g) haricots verts
(or thin green beans)
½ cup (125 mL) spiced pecans
1 Tbsp (15 mL) sweet butter

Prepare a bowl of ice water.

Bring a large stockpot filled with water to a boil then add the 2 Tbsp (30 mL) coarse salt. Carefully add the beans to the stockpot and cook for 2–3 minutes. Remove with a wire strainer and transfer to the bowl of ice water to stop the cooking process. In a sauté pan over low heat add the blanched beans, spiced pecans and sweet butter. Heat the beans through. The butter should form a creamy coating. Remove from the heat and keep warm until needed.

For the spiced pecans

1 tsp (5 mL) sweet butter
1 cup (250 mL) extra-large pecans
1 tsp (5 mL) smoky rub (recipe page 126)
2 Tbsp (30 mL) maple syrup
1 tsp (5 mL) coarse salt

Preheat oven to 300°F (150°C).

In a large sauté pan over medium heat, melt the butter. Add the pecans and smoky rub and stir to coat. Add the maple syrup and cook until the pecans are completely coated. Remove from the heat and transfer to a non-stick sheet pan. Bake on the middle rack in the oven, stirring frequently with a wooden spoon to keep the pecans from sticking together. This process should take 10–12 minutes. When dry and free-moving, remove the pecans from the heat and transfer the baking pan to a wire rack to cool completely. Sprinkle with salt and transfer to a bowl and store uncovered until needed.

For the bovine vinaigrette

1 shallot, peeled and thinly sliced
½ cup (125 mL) extra virgin olive oil
¼ cup (60 mL) sherry vinegar
¼ cup (60 mL) veal jus (recipe page 150)
½ tsp (2 mL) thyme leaves
coarse salt
freshly ground black pepper

In a large nonreactive bowl, combine the shallot, olive oil, sherry vinegar, veal stock and thyme leaves. Adjust the seasoning with salt and pepper. Cover and refrigerate until ready to use. Remove 10–15 minutes before ready to use.

When ready to serve

Divide the haricots verts and spiced pecans evenly in the center of 4 warm dinner plates. Slice the veal rib eye into 4 equal portions and place on top of the haricots verts. Use your hands to carefully place the shoestring potatoes to the side of the veal. Bovine vinaigrette is best served on the side and poured over the veal just before eating.

pork tenderloin

cinnamon roasted carrots | onion crêpes | cider vinegar sauce

This is one of those "feel good" dishes. It's a close tie between the smell of cinnamon and the thought that you're having a breakfast item for dinner.

To build the dish
pork tenderloin
pork rub
cinnamon roasted carrots
onion crêpes
caramelized onions
cider vinegar sauce

Serves 4

For the pork tenderloin

2 pork tenderloins, center cut, about 1 lb (500 g) each
1 Tbsp (15 mL) vegetable oil
coarse salt
freshly ground black pepper

Preheat oven to 375°F (190°C). Place a wire rack on a sheet pan.

Rub the pork tenderloins with the vegetable oil and season with salt and pepper. In a cast iron frying pan over medium-high heat sear the pork tenderloins on all sides until well caramelized, about 4–5 minutes. Remove from the heat and transfer to a clean work surface. Brush with pork rub until well coated, transfer to the prepared sheet pan and place on the middle rack of the oven. Roast until medium rare, about 6–7 minutes. Remove from the heat, and brush with any remaining pork rub. Loosely cover with foil, reserve and keep warm until needed.

For the pork rub

3 Tbsp (45 mL) blackstrap molasses
1 tsp (5 mL) smoked paprika
pinch of cayenne pepper
½ tsp (2 mL) black pepper
½ tsp (2 mL) ground cumin
1 lemon, zest only

In a small saucepan over low heat combine all the pork rub ingredients. Gently simmer until aromatic, about 2–3 minutes. Remove from the heat, transfer to a nonreactive container and cool completely. Refrigerate, covered.

For the cinnamon roasted carrots

2 bunches baby carrots, washed and peeled
2–3 cinnamon sticks
1 Tbsp (15 mL) sweet butter

Preheat oven to 350°F (180°C).

In a small ovenproof baking dish combine the carrots, cinnamon sticks and butter. Place on the middle rack of the oven and roast until lightly caramelized, about 20–25 minutes. Remove from the heat and keep warm until needed.

For the onion crêpes

2 large eggs
3 large egg yolks
1⅓ cups (325 mL) 2% milk
¼ cup plus 1 Tbsp (75 mL) sweet butter, melted
1 cup (250 mL) all-purpose flour
coarse salt
freshly ground white pepper
about 2 Tbsp (30 mL) clarified butter
1 cup (250 mL) caramelized onions

Line a sheet pan with parchment paper.

Whisk together the eggs and egg yolks. Set aside.

Heat the milk in a small saucepan over low heat until just warm. Add the melted butter then slowly whisk the egg mixture into the flour. When blended, strain through a fine mesh sieve and set aside to rest at room temperature for at least 1 hour. Preheat a crêpe pan over medium heat and brush with the clarified butter. Stir the crêpe batter. If it's thicker than whipping cream, thin it with milk, a teaspoon at a time. When the butter is very hot, but not brown, lift the pan off the heat and ladle in the batter. Quickly tilt the pan so that the batter lightly covers the bottom of the pan. Return the pan to the heat. If the batter is of the right consistency and the pan is hot enough, the crêpe will set immediately and will take about 1 minute for the bottom to brown lightly. Use your fingers to pick up the edge to check for browning. Shake the pan back and forth to keep the crêpe from sticking.

When the crêpe bottom is lightly browned, flip it over and cook for 30 seconds. As each crêpe is cooked, turn it out onto a clean kitchen towel. Continue buttering the pan and cooking crêpes until all the batter is used up. Transfer to the prepared sheet pan and keep warm until needed.

For the caramelized onions

2 large white onions, peeled and sliced as thinly as possible
1 Tbsp (15 mL) sweet butter
1 tsp (5 mL) fresh thyme leaves
½ cup (125 mL) sherry
coarse salt
freshly ground black pepper

In a large sauté pan over low heat sauté the sliced onions in the butter until deep brown, about 20 minutes. Add the thyme and deglaze with the sherry. Continue to cook until all the liquid has evaporated. Season to taste with salt and pepper. Remove from the heat and keep warm until needed.

For the cider vinegar sauce

½ cup (125 mL) dried apples, finely diced
1 Tbsp (15 mL) sweet butter
1 tsp (5 mL) Dijon mustard
½ cup (125 mL) cider vinegar
1 cup (250 mL) veal demi-glace (recipe page 150)

In a medium-sized saucepan over low heat sauté the dried apples in the butter until soft, about 4–5 minutes. Add the Dijon mustard and stir to evenly coat the apples. Deglaze with the vinegar and veal demi-glace, continuing to cook until well combined. Remove from the heat and keep warm until needed.

When ready to serve

Divide the roasted carrots evenly in the center of 4 warm dinner plates. Carve the pork tenderloins into ¼-inch (0.5-cm) slices and place to the side of the carrots. On a clean work surface place the crêpes with the lightest colored side facing up. Divide the caramelized onions into the bottom right of the crêpe. Fold the crêpe in half and half again to form a triangle. Place the crêpe, open-side up, against the sliced pork. Drizzle with cider vinegar sauce.

lamb shank

saffron pearls | parsnip crisps | fig paint

Lamb shanks are one of my favorite things to cook when it starts to get cool, not only because of the awesome flavors, but also because your home smells so great as you cook. I eat this dish with a simple seasonal salad. Don't mess with greatness!

To build the dish
lamb shanks
braising liquid
saffron pearls
parsnip crisps
fig paint

Serves 4

For the lamb shanks

4 hind lamb shanks, frenched, about 14–16 oz (400–450 g)
freshly ground black pepper
coarse salt
2 Tbsp (30 mL) vegetable oil

Season the lamb shanks with salt and pepper. Heat the vegetable oil in a heavy-bottomed frying pan over medium-high heat. Sear the shanks on all sides until evenly caramelized. Remove from the heat and reserve.

For the braising liquid

2 Tbsp (30 mL) olive oil
1 medium onion, peeled and diced
2 Roma tomatoes, halved and seeded
1 cup (250 mL) dried figs
½ bunch oregano, picked and stems discarded
6 cloves garlic
½ tsp (2 mL) dried chilies
1 lemon, juice only
1 cup (250 mL) dry white wine

Preheat oven to 300°F (150°C).

In a large stockpot big enough to hold the lamb shanks, heat the olive oil over medium heat. Add the onion and sweat until clear, about 3 minutes. Add the tomatoes, figs, oregano, garlic and chilies, and continue to sauté, stirring until aromatic, about 3 minutes. Deglaze with the lemon juice and white wine. Add the lamb shanks and enough water to cover completely. Bring this to a simmer, uncovered. Turn off the heat, cover and transfer to the oven. Braise until the meat is fork tender and loose on the bone, about 2½ hours. Remove from the oven and cool completely in the braising liquid. Carefully remove the shanks and reserve, covered. Return the braising liquid to the stovetop over medium heat and reduce by half, checking the flavor often. Do not season with salt until the desired consistency has been obtained. Remove from the heat and keep warm until needed. Place the lamb shanks on a sheet pan then use a pastry brush to coat the shanks with fig paint. Continue until all the paint is used. Transfer to a warm oven for about 5–7 minutes to candy the fig paint on the shank.

For the saffron pearls

1 shallot, peeled and minced
2 Tbsp (30 mL) sweet butter
1 Tbsp (15 mL) extra virgin olive oil
½ tsp (2 mL) saffron threads
1 cup (250 mL) acini de pepe pasta
coarse salt
6 cups (1.5 L) vegetable stock (recipe page 150)

In a large saucepan over medium heat, sweat the shallot with 1 Tbsp (15 mL) of the butter and the olive oil until translucent, about 3 minutes. Add the saffron and continue to cook for another minute. Add the pasta, salt and vegetable stock. Bring to a boil, stirring to ensure the pasta doesn't stick to the bottom of the pot. Reduce the heat to low and cover. Continue to cook until the pasta is al dente, about 5–7 minutes. Remove from the heat, drain and transfer to a small saucepan with the remaining tablespoon of butter. Stir until well coated to help prevent the pasta from sticking. Cover and reserve until needed.

lamb shank (continued)

For the parsnip crisps

4 large parsnips, washed and peeled
vegetable oil for frying
coarse salt

Preheat deep-fryer to 375°F (190°C). Line a bowl with paper towel.

On a Japanese mandoline set as thin as possible, slice the parsnips lengthwise. Continue until all the parsnips have been sliced. Using your hands, gently separate the parsnip slices and carefully drop them into the fryer in small batches. Use a slotted spoon to separate the parsnip strips while they fry. Fry until golden brown, about 3–4 minutes. Remove from the deep-fryer and transfer to the prepared bowl. Season with salt and reserve until needed.

For the fig paint

1 cup (250 mL) dried figs
2 Tbsp (30 mL) brown sugar
2 Tbsp (30 mL) balsamic vinegar
4 cups (1 L) apple juice

In a small saucepan over low heat combine all the fig paint ingredients and bring to a simmer. Continue to cook until reduced to 1/4 of the original volume. Remove from the heat and transfer to a food processor fitted with a metal blade. Purée until smooth. The paint should have the consistency of jam. If it looks too thin, return it to the heat and reduce again until the proper consistency is achieved.

When ready to serve

Divide the saffron pearls evenly in the center of 4 warm dinner plates and top each with a lamb shank. Use your hands to gently place equal amounts of parsnip crisps to the side. Brush the shanks with any remaining fig paint.

black cod

sweet potato | collard greens | shrimp gumbo

Black cod, also called sablefish, is coat-your-mouth fish flavor without being overpowering. This is fish lovers' fish.

To build the dish
bacon-wrapped black cod
sweet potato purée
collard greens
shrimp gumbo
broiled shrimp

Serves 4

For the bacon-wrapped black cod

4 fillets black cod, about 5–6 oz (150–175 g) each
8 strips double-smoked slab bacon (sliced as thinly as possible)
8–12 sprigs flat-leaf parsley, stems removed
1 Tbsp (15 mL) smoky rub (recipe page 126)
coarse salt
freshly ground black pepper
1 Tbsp (15 mL) olive oil

Preheat oven to 325°F (160°C). Line a sheet pan with parchment paper.

Place a 12-inch (30-cm) square piece of plastic wrap on a clean, flat work surface. In the center place 2 strips of bacon. On one end of the strips place 1 piece of cod and 2–3 leaves of parsley. Sprinkle with smoky rub. Roll the cod in the bacon, keeping the plastic on the outside. Twist the ends to make a tight package. Repeat for the remaining portions. Refrigerate until needed. Remove the plastic wrap from the cod and season with salt and pepper. Rub with the olive oil. In a large sauté pan over medium heat, sear the cod on all sides until lightly colored. Transfer to the prepared sheet pan and roast until firm to the touch, about 8–10 minutes. Remove and keep warm until needed.

For the sweet potato purée

2 large sweet potatoes
2 large Yukon gold potatoes
1 cup (250 mL) whipping (35%) cream
1 vanilla pod, split
¼ cup (60 mL) sweet butter
coarse salt
freshly ground white pepper

Preheat oven to 400°F (200°C).

Wash and pierce the sweet potatoes, place on a small sheet pan and transfer to the oven. Bake until soft to the touch, about 45 minutes. Remove from the oven and let cool until you can handle them. Peel and discard the skins then pass them through a food mill or ricer. Cover with plastic wrap and reserve. Peel the Yukon gold potatoes and cut them in half. Place in a small saucepan with enough water to cover. Bring to a boil and cook until the potatoes slip off a small paring knife. Remove from the heat, drain and place on a small sheet pan. Transfer to a warm oven to dry slightly, about 5 minutes. Remove from the oven and pass through a food mill or ricer. Cover with plastic wrap and reserve.

In a small saucepan over medium heat, bring the whipping cream and vanilla pod to a boil. Reduce the heat to a simmer and continue cooking for 5 minutes. Remove from the heat and reserve. In a small saucepan over high heat, cook the butter until foamy and a nutty aroma has developed. Remove from the heat and stop the cooking process with the cream mixture. In a large pot over low heat, combine both the potatoes and the butter-cream mixture. Mix with a wooden spoon until combined. Season to taste with salt and pepper. Remove from the heat, cover and reserve.

black cod (continued)

For the collard greens

1 small bunch collard greens
1 Tbsp (15 mL) olive oil
½ cup (125 mL) diced chorizo sausage
1 shallot, peeled and sliced thinly
coarse salt
freshly ground black pepper

Prepare a bowl of ice water.

Remove the large center vein from the collard greens. Wash thoroughly in cold water. Drain and cut into 2-inch (5-cm) squares. In a large pot of lightly salted boiling water, cook the collards for 5 minutes. Remove with a wire strainer and plunge into the ice water. Remove and squeeze out as much excess water as possible. In a large sauté pan over medium heat, add the olive oil, chorizo and shallot. Sauté until soft, about 2 minutes. Add the collards and continue to cook, combining the shallot evenly. Season with salt and pepper. Remove from the heat and keep warm until needed.

For the shrimp gumbo

1 small red pepper, seeded and chopped
1 small green pepper, seeded and chopped
1 rib celery, washed and chopped
1 small onion, peeled and chopped
4 cloves garlic, peeled and chopped
1 bay leaf
1 Tbsp (15 mL) sweet butter
1 Tbsp (15 mL) smoky rub (recipe page 126)
1 cup (250 mL) veal jus (recipe page 150)
1 cup (250 mL) shellfish stock (recipe page 149)
1 bottle dark beer
¼ cup (60 mL) sherry
2 Tbsp (30 mL) dark roux (recipe page 149)
coarse salt
freshly ground black pepper

In a large stockpot over high heat, sauté the peppers, celery, onion, garlic and bay leaf in the butter for 10 minutes. Add the veal jus, shellfish stock, beer and sherry. Reduce the heat and cook until reduced by half, about 30 minutes. Add the roux and continue to cook for 10 minutes. Adjust seasoning with salt and pepper. Remove from the heat and purée in a commercial bar blender in small batches. Pass through a fine mesh sieve and keep warm until needed.

For the broiled shrimp

8 large black tiger shrimp
1 Tbsp (15 mL) olive oil
1 tsp (5 mL) white fish rub (see page 150)

Preheat broiler to 500°F (260°C).

Split and devein the shrimp, keeping the shell intact. Lay flat on a small sheet pan. Drizzle with olive oil and broil for 3–4 minutes. Remove from the heat and sprinkle with white fish rub and keep warm until needed.

When ready to serve

Divide the collard greens equally in the center of 4 warm dinner plates. Slice the roasted cod fillets in half and place on either side of the collard greens. Place the warm sweet potato purée in a pastry bag fitted with a large plain tip. Pipe about ¼ of the purée up against the cod. Top each cod with 2 broiled shrimp. Pool some shrimp gumbo on each plate.

T UP!
THAI

flounder

chorizo | masa dumplings | vegetable escabèche

I normally use this vegetable escabèche with pan-fried fish but I find using a bamboo steamer for the flounder produces a considerably lighter dish.

To build the dish
white fish broth
flounder
chorizo sausage
masa dumplings
vegetable escabèche
escabèche vinaigrette

Serves 4

For the white fish broth

2–3 lb (1–1.5 kg) white fish bones, like flounder, sole or halibut
coarse salt
1 head celery, washed and chopped
1 white onion, peeled and chopped
2 cloves garlic, peeled and minced
2 fresh bay leaves
1 Tbsp (15 mL) white peppercorns
24 cups (6 L) water

Prepare a sink of ice water.

In a large bowl, sprinkle the fish bones with a generous amount of salt and run under cold water to remove any blood. This should take about 20 minutes. Drain and place in a large stockpot with the remaining ingredients. Bring to a very gentle simmer. Remove any foam that may surface with a ladle. Simmer until aromatic, about 30 minutes. Remove from the heat and cool the stockpot in ice water. Transfer to a plastic container, cover and refrigerate until needed.

For the flounder

4 flounder fillets about 6 oz (170 g) each
1 Tbsp (15 mL) sweet butter
1 tsp (5 mL) smoked paprika
2 limes, sliced as thinly as possible
coarse salt

Place the fillets on a clean work surface, skinned side down. With your hands, work the butter and smoked paprika into a smooth paste on the cutting board. Gently rub over the fillets. Cover the bottom of a large bamboo steamer with the sliced limes. Lay the fillets on the lime slices and season with salt. Place the lid on and transfer to a stockpot with the simmering white fish broth. Steam until just firm to the touch, about 4 minutes. Remove from the heat and reserve.

For the chorizo sausage

2 cured chorizo sausages
1 Tbsp (15 mL) extra virgin olive oil
coarse salt as needed
freshly ground black pepper

This only works if the sausage is very dry, almost hard. Ask your butcher when you buy the sausage to put it on the meat slicer and shave it lengthwise as thinly as possible. When ready to serve, brush with olive oil and season with salt and pepper.

For the masa dumplings

- ¾ cup (175 mL) masa harina
- ⅔ cup (150 mL) warm water
- 2 Tbsp (30 mL) extra virgin olive oil
- ½ tsp (2 mL) coarse salt
- 4 cups (1 L) white fish broth

In a large bowl knead together all the ingredients except the white fish broth until combined. Roll into 12 balls, cover and set aside. Bring the white fish stock to a gentle simmer then add the dumplings one at a time. Cover and simmer for 5 minutes. Remove from the heat and keep warm until ready to use.

For the vegetable escabèche

- 2–3 stalks heart of palm, cut into ¼-inch (0.5-cm) medallions
- 1 ruby red grapefruit, peeled and sectioned
- 1 small red onion, peeled and sliced paper-thin
- 1 small yellow pepper, cut in half, seeds and stem discarded, sliced paper-thin
- 1 oz (25 g) ginger, peeled and sliced paper-thin
- 2 oz (50 g) jicama, peeled and sliced paper-thin
- 1 small poblano pepper, sliced paper-thin
- ½ cup (125 mL) cilantro leaves, washed
- ½ cup (125 mL) mint leaves
- ½ cup (125 mL) escabèche vinaigrette
- coarse salt as needed
- freshly ground black pepper

In a large nonreactive bowl, gently mix together all the ingredients, except the salt and pepper, until evenly coated. Season with salt and pepper and let stand at room temperature for 30 minutes. Cover and refrigerate if not using immediately.

For the escabèche vinaigrette

- 2 large shallots, peeled and sliced
- pinch of saffron
- 1 Tbsp (15 mL) olive oil
- 1 cup (250 mL) sherry
- ½ cup (125 mL) sherry vinegar
- 1 jalapeño pepper, split and seeds discarded
- 1 cinnamon stick
- 12 allspice berries
- 3 cans coconut milk
- 1 tsp (5 mL) salt

In a small sauté pan over medium heat, sauté the shallots and saffron in the olive oil until the shallots are translucent, about 3 minutes. Carefully deglaze with the sherry and sherry vinegar. Add the jalapeño, cinnamon stick and allspice berries and continue to simmer. Reduce until almost dry. Add the coconut milk and bring to a boil. Continue to cook for 5 minutes. Remove from the heat and adjust the seasoning with salt. Pass through a fine mesh strainer and transfer to a nonreactive container to cool. Refrigerate, covered, until ready to use.

When ready to serve

Divide the vegetable escabèche equally in the center of 4 warm dinner bowls. Place 2 slices of chorizo sausage on 1 side of the escabèche and 3 masa dumplings on the other. Top with the steamed flounder and drizzle with escabèche vinaigrette.

skate wings

beets | sea beans | potato sails

This ray was once a throwaway, but all you have to do is taste it and you'll be as hooked as I am. It's great for kids because it has no bones.

To build the dish
skate wings
golden beets
sea beans
potato sails

Serves 4

For the skate wings

4 skate wings about ½ lb (225 g) each
1 Tbsp (15 mL) all-purpose flour
coarse salt
freshly ground white pepper
2 Tbsp (30 mL) sweet butter
1 lemon, juice only

Dust the skate wings with flour. Season with salt and white pepper, and reserve. In a large sauté pan over medium-high heat warm the butter until it starts to foam. Add the skate wings and cook until crisp and golden brown, about 3–4 minutes per side. If the skate is getting too brown, reduce the heat but continue to cook. When the skate is firm to the touch, deglaze the pan with the lemon juice. Remove from the pan, pour the pan drippings over the skate, reserve and keep warm until needed.

For the golden beets

4–6 medium-sized golden beets
2 cups (500 mL) coarse salt
1 Tbsp (15 mL) sweet butter
freshly grated nutmeg, to taste

Preheat oven to 325°F (160°C). Cover the bottom of a small sheet pan with an even layer of coarse salt.

Trim the beet greens to about 1 inch (2.5 cm) from the bulb and wash the greens in cold running water until all the dirt is gone. Wash the bulbs thoroughly under running water until all the debris is removed and reserve until plating.

Place the cleaned beets on the prepared pan of salt and transfer to the middle rack of the oven. Roast until soft to the touch, about 30–45 minutes depending on the size of the beets. Remove from the heat and cool until you can hold them comfortably in your hands. Use a clean towel to gently rub the outer skin off the beets. Trim the tops and the root tail off the beets and slice ⅛ inch (3 mm) thick.

In a small sauté pan over low heat, gently warm the butter until it just melts. Add the sliced beets and gently toss until well coated. Season with freshly grated nutmeg. The beets should pick up enough salt from the roasting, but if not, don't worry, the sea beans will pack a salty punch! Remove from the heat and keep warm until needed.

skate wings (continued)

For the sea beans

1 cup (250 mL) sea beans
1 Tbsp (15 mL) sweet butter

In a large pot of boiling water blanch the sea beans for 3–4 minutes. Remove with a slotted spoon and transfer to a small sauté pan over low heat. Add the sweet butter and heat until it just melts. Remove from the heat and keep warm until needed.

For the potato sails

2 medium-sized Yukon gold potatoes
1 Tbsp (15 mL) clarified butter
coarse salt

Preheat oven to 375°F (190°C). Line a sheet pan with a silicone baking mat.

Peel the potatoes, keeping their barrel shape. On a Japanese mandoline, slice the potatoes as thinly as possible into a large nonreactive bowl with the melted butter. Toss the potato slices until evenly coated then place on the prepared sheet pan, overlapping to form a 2 x 8-inch (5 x 20-cm) rectangular sail, about 16 potato slices. Continue until you have 4 sails. Place another silicone baking mat on top and cover with another sheet pan. Transfer to the middle rack of the oven and bake until golden brown, about 20–25 minutes depending on the thickness of the potatoes. Check on the potatoes every 5 minutes or so until done. Remove from the heat and cool completely.

When ready to serve

Divide the beets and beet greens equally in the center of 4 warm dinner plates. Place a skate wing directly on top and drizzle with any remaining pan drippings. Top with sea beans and potato sails.

monkfish

crab sticks | fat noodles | chili hot pot

Monkfish is one of the creepiest fish in the world to clean. I hope you never have to do it. Sometimes called the poor man's lobster, what it lacks in looks, it makes up for in flavor. I would happily eat this any day of the week, as long as I'm not the one cleaning it, of course!

To build the dish
monkfish tails
Asian fish rub
crab sticks
Chinese fat noodles
chili hot pot

Serves 4

For the monkfish tails

4 monkfish tails, skinned with bone still in, about 10 oz (300 g) each
1 Tbsp (15 mL) canola oil
1 tsp (5 mL) Szechuan peppercorns, crushed
coarse salt
2 Tbsp (30 mL) Asian fish rub

Preheat oven to 350°F (180°C). Line a sheet pan with parchment paper.

Rub the tails with the canola oil. Season with pepper and salt. In a large sauté pan over medium-high heat, sear the tails on all surfaces. Remove from the heat and transfer to the prepared sheet pan. Brush with Asian fish rub until well coated. Roast until firm to the touch, about 10 minutes depending on the size of the tails. Remove from the heat and rest in a warm place until needed.

For the Asian fish rub

1 Tbsp (15 mL) ginger, peeled and chopped
1 Tbsp (15 mL) garlic, peeled and chopped
1 cup (250 mL) loosely packed cilantro leaves
1 Thai bird chili, split, seeded and chopped
1 tsp (5 mL) sesame oil
¼ cup (60 mL) canola oil

In a food processor fitted with a metal blade, pulse all the ingredients into a smooth paste. Remove to a plastic container and refrigerate until needed.

For the crab sticks

3 cloves garlic, peeled and minced
½ tsp (2 mL) ginger, peeled and minced
2 Tbsp (30 mL) peanut oil
½ cup (125 mL) ground pork
1 tsp (5 mL) fish sauce
½ tsp (2 mL) freshly ground black pepper
½ tsp (2 mL) coarse salt
½ tsp (2 mL) cornstarch
1½ cups (375 mL) jumbo lump crab meat
1 packet spring roll wrappers
1½ tsp (7 mL) cornstarch dissolved in 2 Tbsp (30 mL) water
vegetable oil for deep-frying

In a large wok over medium-low heat, stir-fry the garlic and ginger in the peanut oil until the garlic is golden, but not burnt. Add the pork and stir-fry for about 1 minute. Add the fish sauce, pepper, salt and ½ tsp (2 mL) of cornstarch. Stir until the cornstarch begins to thicken the mixture, about 2 minutes. Add the crab, quickly toss to incorporate then remove from the heat and let cool.

Preheat deep-fryer to 375°F (190°C).

Separate the spring roll wrappers and set aside. Arrange the individual spring roll wrapper so it looks like a diamond as you face it. Baste the perimeter with about a 1-inch (2.5-cm) ribbon of the dissolved cornstarch. Place a spoonful of filling along the bottom portion of the wrapper. Pull the bottom point up to cover the filling then fold in both sides to meet in the center. Continue rolling and seal the top flap. Repeat with each wrapper and set aside, covered with a damp kitchen towel. The finished rolls should have a uniform, cylindrical shape. Deep-fry the rolls in batches in the vegetable oil, until each one is crispy and golden. Remove and drain on paper towels. Keep warm until needed.

For the Chinese fat noodles

- 3 cups (750 mL) all-purpose flour
- 1 cup (250 mL) cold water
- 1 Tbsp (15 mL) corn oil

Line a sheet pan with parchment paper.

Place the flour in a food processor fitted with a metal blade and, with the motor running, add the water all at once. Process until smooth, about 3–4 minutes. Remove and place the dough in a large bowl, cover it with a damp towel, then loosely cover with a piece of plastic wrap and set aside at room temperature for 1–2 hours so the gluten in the dough relaxes.

Lightly flour your work surface and roll out the dough into a ¼-inch (0.5-cm) thick rectangle. Sprinkle the surface of the dough lightly with flour and fold the rectangle in half to form a smaller rectangle. With a sharp knife, cut the dough into ¼-inch (0.5-cm) wide strips. Place the noodles on the prepared sheet pan. Sprinkle them lightly with flour and separate them with your hands. Cover with a clean kitchen towel.

Bring a large pot of water to a boil over high heat. Add the oil and noodles and cook for 3–5 minutes. Taste one of the noodles to make sure the center is cooked but still firm to the bite. When the noodles are cooked scoop them out with a Chinese strainer and place in a colander to finish draining. Transfer to a clean work surface and cool completely before transferring them to a container. Refrigerate, covered, until needed.

For the chili hot pot

- 1 Tbsp (15 mL) vegetable oil
- 2 lb (1 kg) shrimp, peeled and deveined (keep the shells)
- 8 cups (2 L) shellfish stock (recipe page 149)
- 1½ tsp (7 mL) coarse salt
- 3 stalks lemon grass, cut into 3-inch (7.5-cm) lengths
- 4 kaffir lime leaves
- 2 Thai bird chilies
- 1 Tbsp (15 mL) fish sauce
- 2 limes, juice only
- ½ bunch cilantro leaves, washed
- 3 scallions, coarsely chopped

Heat the oil in a large saucepan over high heat and fry the reserved shrimp shells until they turn pink. Add the shellfish stock, salt, lemon grass, kaffir lime leaves and chilies. Bring to a boil, cover, reduce the heat and simmer for 20 minutes. Strain the mixture through a sieve, return the liquid to a saucepan and bring to a boil. Remove from the heat and cool completely.

When ready to serve

Bring the chili hot pot to a boil in a large saucepan over high heat. Reduce the heat to a simmer and add the Chinese noodles. Bring back to a simmer, about 2 minutes. Add the shrimp and cook for 2 minutes. Remove from the heat to prevent overcooking and add the fish sauce, lime juice, cilantro and scallions. Divide the broth into 4 warm dinner bowls and place monkfish tails in the broth. Garnish with crab sticks and serve piping hot.

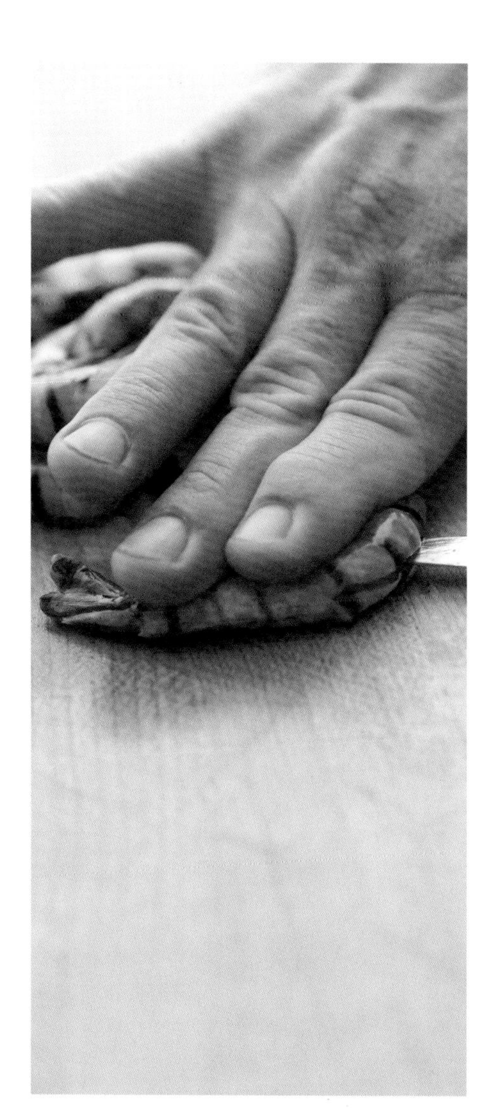

duck "twofer"

roasted magret breast | confit leg

This dish was inspired by the wonderful moulard duck. These ducks are primarily used for the production of foie gras and you will always find a little foie gras treasure in my duck dishes.

To build the dish
roasted duck breast
duck leg confit
duck confit seasoning
glazed parsnips
wild rice dumplings
Brussels sprout hash
aspiration
cloudberry jus

Serves 4

For the roasted duck breast

2 moulard duck breasts about 10 oz (300 g) each
coarse salt
freshly ground black pepper

Preheat oven to 375°F (190°C).

Score the skin of the duck breast in a ¼-inch (0.5-cm) cross-hatched pattern. Season the flesh side with salt and pepper. Place the duck breast skin side down in a cool sauté pan and place over low heat. Cook the breast slowly for 8–10 minutes, this will help render out most of the fat. Carefully turn the breast and sear the flesh side for 2 minutes. Remove from the pan, place on a sheet pan and transfer to the middle rack of the oven. Roast until firm to the touch, about 7–10 minutes. Remove from the oven and rest in a warm place until needed.

For the duck leg confit

4 small duck legs
2 Tbsp (30 mL) coarse salt
1 Tbsp (15 mL) duck confit seasoning
6 cups (1.5 L) duck fat or vegetable oil

Rub the duck legs with salt and confit seasoning and place on a small tray. Refrigerate, uncovered, for a good portion of the day, about 6 hours. This will help remove some of the moisture in the duck. Remove from the refrigerator and brush off most of the seasoning.

Preheat oven to 275°F (140°C).

Neatly pack the duck legs in a small oven-proof dish and cover with fat then parchment paper then aluminum foil. Bake for 3 hours. Remove from the oven and let cool in the fat. Transfer to the refrigerator and store, covered, until needed.

For the duck confit seasoning

1½ Tbsp (17 mL) ground black pepper
1½ Tbsp (17 mL) ground ginger
1 Tbsp (15 mL) ground corriander
1 tsp (5 mL) ground nutmeg
1 tsp (5 mL) ground cinnamon
1 tsp (5 mL) ground cumin
1 tsp (5 mL) ground clove

Mix all the ingredients together and store in an airtight container.

duck "twofer" (continued)

For the glazed parsnips

4–6 parsnips, peeled and cut on a bias
1 Tbsp (15 mL) grape seed oil
coarse salt

In a small sauté pan over medium-low heat, cook the parsnips in the grape seed oil. Stir to achieve an even golden brown color, about 7 minutes. Season with salt and remove from the heat. Keep warm until needed.

For the wild rice dumplings

2 cups (500 mL) all-purpose flour (plus 2 cups/500 mL for kneading)
1 cup (250 mL) 2% milk
2 large eggs
1 Tbsp (15 mL) baking powder
½ cup (125 mL) cooked wild rice
1 small onion, minced and browned
1 tsp (5 mL) fresh thyme, chopped
coarse salt
freshly ground black pepper
2–3 oz (50–70 g) foie gras, sautéed
vegetable oil, for frying

Preheat deep-fryer to 350°F (180°C).

In a large mixing bowl, combine the flour, milk, eggs and baking powder. Mix with a wooden spoon until a soft dough has formed. Add the wild rice and onion and mix until evenly distributed in the dough. Season with salt and pepper. Turn the dough onto a heavily floured work surface. Knead the dough until it's very firm and almost all the flour is incorporated, about 6–8 minutes. Cover tightly with plastic wrap so it doesn't dry out while you work. Divide the dough into 12 pieces and roll out into small circles about 3 inches (7.5 cm) in diameter. Break off a small piece of foie gras the size of a grape and place in the center of each circle. Fold over to create half circles and press the edges down. Blanch in salted boiling water for 1–2 minutes, remove and drain on a clean kitchen towel. Cover and refrigerate until needed. Deep-fry until golden brown, about 3–4 minutes. Remove and drain on paper towels.

For the Brussels sprout hash

16–20 Brussels sprouts
4 strips double-smoked bacon, cut into lardons
2 shallots, peeled and sliced paper-thin
1 Tbsp (15 mL) sweet butter
¼ cup (60 mL) white wine
coarse salt
freshly ground black pepper

Peel the tough or blemished outer leaves from the sprouts. Holding the stem of each sprout, slice as thinly as possible on a Japanese mandoline. Discard the stem. In a large sauté pan over medium heat, render the bacon until crisp, about 5 minutes. Drain off any excess fat then add the shallots and butter. Continue to cook until the shallots have softened, about 3 minutes. Add the Brussels sprouts and continue to cook. Deglaze the pan with the white wine. The sprouts are done when they are wilted and bright green. Season to taste with salt and pepper. Remove from the heat and keep warm until needed.

For the aspiration

1 large bunch aspiration, washed and stems peeled
1 Tbsp (15 mL) sweet butter
coarse salt
freshly ground white pepper

Prepare an ice bath.

In a large pot of boiling water, blanch the aspiration for 2 minutes, remove and shock in an ice bath. Drain well. In a small sauté pan over low heat, warm the aspiration. Be careful not to brown the butter. Season with salt and pepper. Reserve and keep warm until needed.

For the cloudberry jus

4 cloves garlic, peeled and minced
1 large shallot, peeled and minced
1 oz (25 g) ginger, peeled and minced
1 orange, zest only
1 lemon, zest only
1 stalk lemon grass, smashed and tied
½ cup (125 mL) cloudberry preserve
¼ cup (60 mL) brandy
1 Tbsp (15 mL) brown sugar
pinch red chili flakes
4 cups (1 L) duck stock (recipe page 149)
¼ cup (60 mL) red wine vinegar
coarse salt
freshly ground black pepper

In a large stockpot over high heat, sauté the garlic, shallots, ginger and orange and lemon zests. Add the lemon grass and continue to cook. Add the cloudberries and bring to a simmer. Add the brandy, brown sugar and chili flakes and stir. Then add the duck stock and vinegar. Reduce the heat and cook until reduced by half, about 30 minutes. Season with salt and pepper. Remove from the heat, strain through a fine china cap and reserve.

When ready to serve

Divide the Brussels sprout hash equally on the side of 4 warm dinner plates. Carve the duck breasts as thinly as possible and place on the hash. Stand 1–2 stems of aspiration to the side of the duck. On the opposite side of the plate equally divide the parsnips and place the duck confit on top. Pool cloudberry jus in opposite corners and place wild rice dumplings on each plate.

squab

corn griddle cake | giblet gravy | caraway cabbage

The first time you eat squab you will probably have a similar experience as I did. I was trying desperately to find a way to tell my chef that the bird was not cooked enough. For his part, he gave me "the look." He explained to me that squab was considered a game bird and it needs to be consumed medium-rare. You only have to try it fully cooked once to understand the wisdom of this.

To build the dish
squab
corn griddle cakes
giblet gravy
caraway cabbage

Serves 4

For the squab

4 squabs, 12–14 oz (400–500 g) each, set aside giblets, livers and necks
1 lemon, zest only
1 tsp (5 mL) thyme leaves
2 cloves garlic, peeled and smashed
2 Tbsp (30 mL) dark corn syrup
1 Tbsp (15 mL) orange marmalade
1 Tbsp (15 mL) bourbon whiskey
coarse salt
freshly ground black pepper

Preheat oven to 350°F (180°C). Place a wire rack over a sheet pan.

Wash and dry the squabs. Remove both the legs and reserve for future use. Use your hands to flip the wings under the body to protect the breasts while roasting. In a small saucepan over low heat bring to a simmer the zest, thyme, garlic, corn syrup, marmalade and bourbon. Simmer until thick and reduced by half, about 3 minutes. Remove from the heat and let cool. Season the inside of the squab cavity and all over the skin with salt and pepper. Use a pastry brush to baste the squab with a generous coating of the marinade. Transfer to the prepared sheet pan and roast on the middle rack of the oven for about 8–10 minutes, until deep brown in color. Remove, cover in aluminum foil and rest in a warm place.

For the corn griddle cakes

1 cup (250 mL) yellow cornmeal
1 tsp (5 mL) granulated sugar
¼ tsp (1 mL) coarse salt
¼ tsp (1 mL) baking soda
1¼ cups (310 mL) buttermilk
1 large egg
2 Tbsp (30 mL) sweet butter, melted
1 Tbsp (15 mL) vegetable oil

In a large bowl, stir together the cornmeal, sugar, salt and baking soda. In a separate bowl, beat together the buttermilk, egg and melted butter. Stir the buttermilk mixture into the dry ingredients until just moistened. Let the batter rest for 30 minutes at room temperature.

Heat the oil in a frying pan and add 2 Tbsp (30 mL) of batter at a time. Cook the griddle cakes on one side until puffed and full of bubbles, looking dry at the edges, then turn and cook for 1 minute or until cooked through. Reserve and keep warm until needed.

For the giblet gravy

6 cups (1.5 L) dark chicken stock
(recipe page 148)
squab giblets, livers and necks
1 small onion, peeled and quartered
1 large carrot, peeled and chopped
2 ribs celery, with leaves
coarse salt to taste
1 Tbsp (15 mL) dark roux (recipe page 149)
1 tsp (5 mL) smoky rub (recipe page 126)
4 hard-boiled quail eggs

In a large stockpot over medium heat bring the stock, giblets, onion, carrot and celery to a boil. As soon as it reaches a boil, reduce the heat and simmer, uncovered, until reduced by half, about 1 hour. Remove from the heat and strain through a fine mesh strainer into a small saucepan then transfer back to the heat. Whisk the dark roux and smoky rub into the simmering stock. If the sauce becomes too thick just thin it down with a little water. Adjust the seasoning with salt if necessary. Set aside the quail eggs until ready to serve.

For the caraway cabbage

1 small Savoy cabbage,
about 4 cups (1 L) cleaned
2 shallots, peeled and sliced
1 Tbsp (15 mL) olive oil
1 tsp (5 mL) caraway seeds
1 Tbsp (15 mL) sweet butter
1 smoked duck breast, shredded
coarse salt
freshly ground black pepper
½ tsp (2 mL) freshly grated nutmeg

Prepare a bowl of ice water. Line a sheet pan with a couple of clean kitchen towels.

Remove the tough outer leaves and quarter the cabbage. Remove the core and cut into 1- x 1-inch (2.5- x 2.5-cm) squares. Use your hands to break the larger cubes into individual layers. Blanch in boiling salted water until just soft, about 2–3 minutes. Remove from the pot and transfer to the bowl of ice water. Drain on the prepared sheet pan.

In a large sauté pan over medium heat sweat the shallots in the olive oil until translucent, about 2 minutes. Add the caraway seeds, butter and blanched cabbage and continue cooking. Reduce the heat to low and add the smoked duck breast. Gently toss until the duck is evenly distributed throughout the cabbage mixture. Season with salt, pepper and nutmeg. Reserve and keep warm until needed.

When ready to serve

Place 2 corn griddle cakes in the center of 4 warm dinner plates and top with caraway cabbage. On a clean work surface carve the squabs in half and place on top of the cabbage. Equally divide the giblet sauce over the squabs and garnish with hard-boiled quail eggs.

turkey

oyster bread pudding | lima beans | white gravy

When I think of turkey I don't usually have the same thoughts as most people do. Not an all-day affair—I want my turkey fast.

To build the dish
turkey breast
turkey rub
oyster bread pudding
lima beans
white gravy

Serves 4

For the turkey breast

1 boneless turkey breast, with skin on, about 2 lb (1 kg)
1 Tbsp (15 mL) turkey rub
2 Tbsp (30 mL) corn oil
coarse salt

Preheat oven to 325°F (160°C). Place a wire rack over a sheet pan.

Tie the turkey breast with butcher's twine at 1-inch (2.5-cm) intervals. Tuck the tip of the breast under your last tie to give you a more even shape. Place the breast on a sheet pan, sprinkle with turkey rub and drizzle with corn oil. Using your hands, pick up the turkey breast and massage in the rub and oil until evenly distributed.

In a large cast iron frying pan over medium heat sear the breast on all sides, being careful not to burn the spice coating. Remove from the frying pan onto the prepared sheet pan and transfer to the middle rack of the oven. Roast until firm to the touch, about 20 minutes. Remove from the oven, cover with aluminum foil and rest. Reserve the pan drippings.

For the turkey rub

1 tsp (5 mL) dried parsley
1 tsp (5 mL) dried sage
1 tsp (5 mL) dried thyme
½ tsp (2 mL) marjoram
½ tsp (2 mL) dried dill

Mix together all the ingredients and store, covered, at room temperature.

For the oyster bread pudding

4 scallions, minced
1 rib celery, peeled to remove strings and diced
1 jalapeño pepper, seeded and minced
3 cloves garlic, peeled and minced
1 Tbsp (15 mL) sweet butter
½ tsp (2 mL) freshly grated nutmeg
1 tsp (5 mL) Old Bay seasoning
1 small yellow pepper, roasted, skinned, seeded and diced
18 oysters
1 cup (250 mL) whipping (35%) cream
3 egg yolks
1 loaf cornbread

Preheat oven to 325°F (160°C).

In a large sauté pan over medium heat sweat the scallions, celery, jalapeño and garlic in the butter until the celery is translucent, about 5 minutes. Add the nutmeg and Old Bay seasoning and continue to cook for another 2 minutes. Add the diced yellow pepper, oysters and any liquid from the bowl, stir to combine and remove from the heat. The heat should just cook the oysters. Transfer to a large mixing bowl and cool completely in the refrigerator. In a small mixing bowl combine the whipping cream and egg yolk and whisk gently. Pour over the oyster mixture and then crumble the cornbread over this. Mix gently until evenly incorporated. Spoon into non-stick muffin tins and bake until deep brown and firm to the touch, about 30 minutes. If the muffins get too dark just cover with aluminum foil while baking. Remove from the heat and keep warm until needed.

For the lima beans

- 2 cups (500 mL) lima beans, blanched and skins removed
- 1 Tbsp (15 mL) sweet butter
- ¼ tsp (1 mL) freshly grated nutmeg
- coarse salt as needed
- freshly grated white pepper
- ½ bunch chervil, stems removed

In a small sauté pan over low heat, warm the lima beans in the butter. You don't want the butter to break so lower the heat if needed. Season with nutmeg, salt and pepper. Remove from the heat, reserve and keep warm until needed. Add the chervil just before serving.

For the white gravy

- 1 Tbsp (15 mL) reserved pan drippings
- 1 cup (250 mL) whipping (35%) cream
- coarse salt
- freshly ground white pepper
- 2 tsp (10 mL) turkey rub
- 1 lemon, zest only

Place the sheet pan you used for the turkey over low heat and add the reserved pan drippings and whipping cream. Season with salt and pepper and reduce the cream until thick, about 5 minutes. Stir in the turkey rub and lemon zest. Simmer until the flavors are blended, about 2 minutes. Remove from the heat, reserve and keep warm until needed.

When ready to serve

Divide the oyster bread pudding equally in the center of 4 warm dinner plates and top with lima beans. On a clean work surface, carve the turkey breast as thinly as possible and place on top of the lima beans. Serve the white gravy on the side.

Cold

December | January | February

When I'm Cold

December | January | February

Over the past years, I've been fortunate to have great opportunities to work in many different and exciting places, honing my skills as a chef. Making a pretty plate of food has its privileges: you get to live and work all over the world. Some memories I particularly cherish are in/of the cities with constant warmth like Los Angeles or constant GO like New York City. As I write this, I chuckle to myself over fond winter memories in Santa Barbara. Cold there meant 82°F, slightly overcast with a light Santa Ana breeze.

Now I'm back in the North East, where cold means losing all feeling from your face muscles, any distance is a justified cab ride away and indoor markets are your best friend. How many times have I wandered through Chinatown in a foot and a half of snow, looking for oxtail?! I have to stop doing that.

As it gets colder, you go from 2-minutes-on-a-grill to 2-hours-in-a-pot cooking. Black-eyed peas find their way from the back of your cupboard to join your black-strap braise. Your patience while baking Old Bay madeleines is rewarded when you taste them with a pimento bisque and West Coast crab.

Short ribs, veal shell steak, venison and whole duck dishes will comfort you despite the cold and intoxicating aromas from a warm oven are guaranteed to keep you cozy.

venison

persimmon brûlée | celery root | port reduction

You don't need to marinade this venison very long because it's one of the most tender cuts of deer. The sweetness of the persimmon brûlée acts as a perfect foil for the meat's slightly gamey taste.

To build the dish
venison
persimmon brûlée
celery root
port reduction

Serves 4

For the venison

1 full rack venison, frenched, about 2 lb (1 kg)
1 lemon, zest only
8–10 juniper berries, crushed
3–4 sprigs thyme
2 cloves garlic, peeled and smashed
1 cup (250 mL) grape seed oil

Combine all the ingredients in a glass baking dish. Cover with plastic wrap and marinate in the refrigerator for 2–3 hours.

Preheat oven to 325°F (160°C). Place a wire rack on a sheet pan. In a cast iron frying pan over medium heat, sear the venison rack on all sides. Remove from the heat and transfer to the prepared sheet pan. Roast on middle rack of the oven until firm to the touch, about 12–15 minutes. Remove from the oven, cover with aluminum foil and rest until needed.

For the persimmon brûlée

2 fuyu persimmons, very soft and ripe
1 Tbsp (15 mL) coarse sugar

Peel the persimmons and chop with a heavy French knife until a purée forms. Divide the purée into 4 portions, spread over clean dinner plates, sprinkle with sugar and heat with a blowtorch until the sugar caramelizes and turns dark brown. Keep the plates off to the side until needed.

For the celery root

1 large celery root, about 2 lb (1 kg)
1 cup (250 mL) whole milk
2 cloves
2 Tbsp (30 mL) sweet butter
coarse salt
freshly ground white pepper as needed

Cut the top off the celery root, creating a flat surface. Use a paring knife to trim the outer layer. Cut into ½-inch (1-cm) slices. Cut the slices into ½-inch (1-cm) wide batons or sticks then trim the sticks into 3-inch (7.5-cm) lengths. Bring the celery batons to a simmer in the milk and cloves. Cook until just tender, about 10 minutes. Remove from the heat and let cool in the cooking liquid. In a small saucepan heat the celery root batons in butter and season with salt and pepper when hot. Remove from the heat and keep warm until needed.

For the port reduction

1 cup (250 mL) port
1 orange, zest only
¼ cup (60 mL) dried cranberries
1 cup (250 mL) veal demi-glace (recipe page 150)
coarse salt

In a small saucepan over medium heat bring the port, orange zest and cranberries to a boil. Reduce slowly until a thick syrup forms, about 20 minutes. Add the veal demi-glace and bring to a boil. Adjust seasoning with salt and remove from the heat. Keep warm until needed.

When ready to serve

Take the plates with the persimmon purée caramelized sugar and spoon some of the celery root to the side. On a clean work surface carve the venison rack into 4 equal portions and place on top of the celery root. To finish, drizzle some port reduction directly over the venison.

veal shell steak

pickled vegetables | kidney hash | horseradish jus

You don't see this cut of steak, sometimes called a Kansas City steak, on very many menus, although any butcher can fabricate the cut. I usually make this dish after a trip to my cantina in the basement in my house, standing in that cold dark room and the only thing left on the shelf is my summertime pickles! This is quick and easy, but very tasty.

To build the dish
veal shell steak
pickled vegetables
kidney hash
horseradish jus

Serves 4

For the veal shell steak

4 veal shell steaks,
 about 12 oz (350 g) each
2 Tbsp (30 mL) olive oil
coarse salt
freshly ground black pepper

Preheat oven to 375°F (190°C). Place a wire rack over a sheet pan.

Drizzle the shell steaks with olive oil and season with salt and pepper. In a large cast iron frying pan over high heat sear the steaks on both sides until caramelized, about 3–4 minutes per side. Remove from the heat and transfer to the prepared sheet pan. Roast on the middle rack of the oven for 10–12 minutes. Remove from the heat and rest in a warm place until needed.

For the pickled vegetables

6 cups (1.5 L) assorted vegetables,
 for example:
 carrots, cut in crinkle coins
 okra
 watermelon rind
 cauliflower
 string beans
1 medium onion, peeled and sliced
1 ½ cups (375 mL) white wine vinegar
1 ½ cups (375 mL) granulated sugar
½ tsp (2 mL) ground turmeric
½ tsp (2 mL) coarse salt
½ tsp (2 mL) white mustard seeds
½ tsp (2 mL) whole celery seeds

Layer the vegetables and onion in a large glass bowl or dish. Combine the remaining ingredients in a small nonreactive saucepan and bring to the boil, swirling the pan occasionally until the sugar is dissolved. Pour the mixture over the vegetables and onion. Allow to cool. Cover tightly with plastic wrap and refrigerate for 24 hours. The pickles will keep for up to 1 month in an airtight container in the refrigerator, or they can be canned using the traditional water-bath method.

For the kidney hash

1 veal kidney, about the size of a clenched fist
1 Tbsp (15 mL) olive oil
6 sprigs flat-leaf parsley, stems removed
3 cloves garlic, peeled and minced
2 Tbsp (30 mL) blackstrap molasses
1 Tbsp (15 mL) butter
1 sweet potato, peeled and diced, about 1 cup (250 mL)
1 poblano pepper, seeded and diced, about ¼ cup (60 mL)
½ cup (125 mL) pearl onions, peeled
½ tsp (2 mL) grated nutmeg
coarse salt
freshly ground black pepper
½ cup (125 mL) veal demi-glace (recipe page 150)

Wash the kidney under cold running water then use your fingers to pick off any remaining suet. Pat dry with a clean kitchen towel. Cut into ½-inch (1-cm) slices and place in a nonreactive bowl with the olive oil, parsley and garlic and gently toss until the kidney slices are coated. In a very hot frying pan, sear the kidney slices on both sides, being careful not to overcook. Remove from the heat, drizzle with molasses and let rest.

In the same frying pan over low heat sauté the sweet potato, poblano pepper and pearl onions in butter until the sweet potato is soft and caramelized. Season with nutmeg, salt and pepper. Add the kidney slices and veal demi-glace. Quickly bring to a boil and adjust the seasoning. Remove from the heat and keep warm until ready to serve.

For the horseradish jus

2–3 oz (50–75 g) fresh horseradish, peeled and grated
1 Tbsp (15 mL) sherry vinegar
½ cup (125 mL) veal jus (recipe page 150)
coarse salt
freshly ground black pepper

In a small saucepan over medium heat sweat the horseradish in the sherry vinegar until soft, about 1 minute. Add the veal jus and bring to a boil. Adjust seasoning with salt and pepper and remove from the heat and keep warm until needed.

When ready to serve

Place a veal shell steak in the center of 4 warm dinner plates. Divide the pickled vegetables and kidney hash across 4 plates and place to the side of the steak. To finish, drizzle each with horseradish jus.

short ribs

black tiger shrimp | black-eyed peas | blackstrap braise

I have jerked almost everything that swims, walks or flies. Usually when you think of jerk you think of the grill but you can be the judge when it comes to tasting this blackstrap braise. I'm sure you'll agree it's the best damned jerk that's never been on the grill.

To build the dish
blackstrap-braised short ribs
black tiger shrimp
black-eyed peas

Serves 4

For the blackstrap-braised short ribs

4 racks beef short ribs, about 1 lb (500 g) each
coarse salt
freshly ground black pepper
¼ cup (60 mL) corn oil
2 Tbsp (30 mL) prepared jerk rub
1 large carrot, peeled and roughly chopped
2 ribs celery, peeled and roughly chopped
1 large onion, peeled and roughly chopped
6 Roma tomatoes, roughly chopped
2 Tbsp (30 mL) honey
4 cups (1 L) veal jus (recipe page 150)
1 bottle (341 mL) dark beer
½ cup (125 mL) sherry
2 bay leaves

Preheat oven to 350°F (180°C).

Season the short ribs with salt and pepper. In a heavy-bottomed saucepan over high heat sear the ribs in corn oil on all sides until evenly caramelized, about 5–6 minutes. Remove the ribs from the pot and coat with jerk rub. Reserve at room temperature until needed.

Return the pot to medium-low heat and sauté the carrot, celery and onion until slightly caramelized and soft, about 5 minutes. Add the tomatoes and continue to cook until they start to break down and become soft, about 10 minutes. Add the honey, veal jus, beer and sherry and bring to a boil. Add the seared ribs and bay leaves. Cover and transfer to the middle rack of the oven.

Braise until the ribs are fork-tender and nearly falling off the bone, about 50 minutes. Remove from the heat and cool completely in the braising liquid. Carefully remove the ribs and strain the liquid then discard the vegetables. Transfer the strained liquid back to the stove and reduce over low heat by half. Pass it through a fine mesh strainer several times until the liquid is clear. Bring the ribs back to a simmer, about 3–4 minutes in the sauce, adjust seasoning if necessary and reserve.

For the black tiger shrimp

4 jumbo black tiger shrimp about 3–4 oz (75–100 g) each
1 Tbsp (15 mL) prepared jerk rub
1 Tbsp (15 mL) corn oil
coarse salt

Preheat broiler. Place a wire rack on a sheet pan.

Carefully peel the tail shells, keeping the fins intact. Use a paring knife to remove the intestinal track then use your fingers to spread the jerk rub into the exposed flesh. Drizzle with the oil, season with salt and transfer to the prepared sheet pan and broil until the flesh is no longer opaque, about 2–3 minutes. Remove from the heat, cover with aluminum foil and keep warm until needed.

short ribs (continued)

For the black-eyed peas

1 cup (250 mL) black-eyed peas, soaked in cold water overnight
4 cups (1 L) vegetable stock (recipe page 150)
½ calabaza pumpkin (or butternut squash) peeled, cut into ¼-inch (0.5-cm) dice
2 Tbsp (30 mL) olive oil
6–8 pods okra, sliced into ¼-inch (0.5-cm) rounds
8 sprigs cilantro, stems discarded and chiffonade
2 scallions, washed and minced
1 lime, juice only
coarse salt
freshly ground black pepper

In a small saucepan over medium heat bring the black-eyed peas to a boil in the vegetable stock. Reduce the heat and simmer until the beans are soft but still retain their shape, about 25 minutes. Remove from the heat and cool completely in the cooking liquid. Drain and reserve.

In a small sauté pan over medium heat sweat the pumpkin in the olive oil until translucent. Add the rest of the ingredients and continue to cook for about 3 minutes. Adjust seasoning to taste and remove from the heat. Keep warm until needed.

When ready to serve

Spoon equal portions of the black-eyed peas in the center of 4 warm dinner plates and place a rack of braised short ribs on top of each. Ladle a generous portion of braising sauce overtop and garnish with jerked black tiger shrimp.

oxtail

red wine ragout | butternut squash ravioli | fried parsley

Oxtail is one of the best bargains to be found in the butcher's shop. Its meat is richly flavored and the gelatin released from the connective tissues enriches it even further after the long slow cooking.

To build the dish
oxtail
red wine ragout
butternut squash ravioli
fried parsley

Serves 4

For the oxtail

3 lb (1.5 kg) oxtail, cut into 3-inch (7.5-cm) pieces
1 Tbsp (15 mL) olive oil
1 onion, peeled and minced
3 cloves garlic, peeled and minced
1 bottle (750 mL) full-bodied red wine
2 cups (500 mL) beef stock (recipe page 148)
1 Tbsp (15 mL) grain mustard
1 lemon, zest only
1 bay leaf
coarse salt as needed

Trim as much excess fat as possible from the oxtail. In a large frying pan over medium heat sear the oxtail pieces in the olive oil until caramelized on all sides, about 5–6 minutes. Remove from the heat and reserve. Add the onion and garlic to the same frying pan and cook until brown but not burnt. Deglaze with the red wine, lifting any bits into the cooking liquid. Add the stock, mustard, zest, bay leaf and reserved oxtail pieces. Bring to a boil. Reduce the heat to a gentle simmer and cook for 3 hours.

Remove from the heat and let cool enough to handle. Pull the meat from the bone and reserve, covered, in the refrigerator. Pass the braising liquid through a fine mesh strainer, cover and transfer to the refrigerator for at least 2 hours.

For the red wine ragout

cooked oxtail
braising liquid
1 cup (250 mL) diced butternut squash
2 large parsnips, peeled and diced
1 large carrot, peeled and diced
2 Tbsp (30 mL) brandy
1 Tbsp (15 mL) brown sugar
3–4 sprigs thyme, stems removed
coarse salt
freshly ground black pepper

In a large saucepan over medium heat bring all the ingredients, except salt and pepper, to a boil. Reduce the heat and simmer until the vegetables are soft but still retain their shape, about 15–20 minutes. Season with salt and pepper and keep warm until needed.

For the butternut squash ravioli

1 lb (500 g) butternut squash
3–4 amaretto cookies
¼ cup (60 mL) grated Parmesan cheese
3–4 sprigs flat-leaf parsley, stems removed
¼ tsp (1 mL) grated nutmeg
coarse salt
freshly ground black pepper
2 cups (500 mL) unbleached all-purpose flour
3 extra-large eggs
2 Tbsp (30 mL) sweet butter

Preheat oven to 400°F (200°C).

Split the butternut squash and scrape out all the seeds. Transfer to a sheet pan and bake for 1 hour. Remove from the heat and let cool. Remove and discard the peel.

In a food processor fitted with a metal blade pulverize the cookies. Add the peeled squash while the motor is running and process until the mixture is smooth. Scrape the filling into a bowl, stir in the Parmesan and nutmeg and season with salt and pepper. Cover and refrigerate until needed.

Put the flour and eggs in the clean food processor and process until the dough forms a ball, about 45 seconds. Remove and keep covered with a damp kitchen towel. Working with half the dough at a time, roll it out to less than 1/16-inch (1-mm) thick. Arrange 1 strip of dough on a clean floured work surface. Drop teaspoonfuls of the squash filling in 2 rows about 3 inches (7.5 cm) apart, down the length of the dough. Drape the second sheet of dough over the filling.

Firmly press around each mound of filling, taking care to press out any trapped air. With a fluted pastry cutter, cut the ravioli into 2-inch (5-cm) squares. Firmly press around the edges to seal them. Cook in a large stockpot of boiling, salted water until just done, about 5–7 minutes. Remove, toss with butter and keep warm until needed.

For the fried parsley

1 bunch flat-leaf parsley, washed and stems removed
vegetable oil for frying
coarse salt

Preheat deep-fryer to 375°F (190°C). Line a bowl with paper towel.

Dry the parsley leaves in a salad spinner, remove and sprinkle into the deep-fryer. Remove when they stop bubbling, about 30 seconds. Transfer to the prepared bowl and season with salt. Keep warm until needed.

When ready to serve

Divide the oxtail ragout, butternut squash ravioli and fried parsley equally in the center of 4 warm dinner bowls.

lamb leg

white cheddar grits | huckleberry jelly | striped beets

I love the flavor of Angostura Bitters and orange with the forward taste of lamb leg.

To build the dish
lamb leg
white cheddar grits
huckleberry jelly
striped beets

Serves 4

For the lamb leg

1 small leg of lamb, deboned, weighing about 3 lb (1.5 kg)
2 Tbsp (30 mL) olive oil
4–5 sprigs thyme
4–5 sprigs oregano
4 cloves garlic, peeled and minced
2 Tbsp (30 mL) ground almonds
coarse salt
freshly ground black pepper
1 orange, juice and zest
1 Tbsp (15 mL) Angostura Bitters

Trim the sinew and excess fat from the lamb leg. In a large nonreactive bowl mix together the oil, thyme, oregano, garlic, almonds, salt and pepper and rub into the lamb. Tie in several places and rub with the orange juice, zest and bitters. Cover and refrigerate for 2–3 hours.

Preheat oven to 350°F (180°C).

Place the lamb in a roasting pan, season with more salt and pepper and roast until firm to the touch, about 1½ hours. Remove and rest in a warm place for 15 minutes before slicing.

For the white cheddar grits

3 cups (750 mL) vegetable stock (recipe page 150)
1 tsp (5 mL) coarse salt
1 cup (250 mL) grits
1 cup (250 mL) sharp white cheddar, grated
coarse salt
freshly ground white pepper

In a large saucepan over high heat bring the stock and salt to a boil. Slowly add the grits, stirring constantly to prevent lumping.

Lower the heat to a gentle simmer and cover the pot. Let the grits simmer, stirring occasionally, for 20 minutes. Stir in the grated cheddar and adjust seasoning with salt and pepper. Remove from the heat and keep warm until needed.

For the huckleberry jelly

½ cup (125 mL) huckleberry jelly
1 Tbsp (15 mL) sherry vinegar

In a small saucepan over low heat melt the jelly and vinegar until smooth. Remove from the heat and keep warm until needed.

For the striped beets

- 1 lb (500 g) striped beets, scrubbed clean
- coarse salt
- 2 Tbsp (30 mL) sweet butter
- 1 Tbsp (15 mL) sherry vinegar
- freshly ground white pepper

Preheat oven to 325°F (160°C). Fill a small baking dish with a 1-inch (2.5-cm) layer of coarse salt.

Wrap the beets in aluminum foil and place in the prepared baking dish. The salt creates even heat in the oven and absorbs any moisture purged from the beets while cooking. Bake until soft to the touch, about 30 minutes, depending on the size of the beets. Remove from the heat and let cool on the salt. Remove the foil then peel and slice the beets 1/8 inch (3 mm) thick. Transfer to a small sauté pan over low heat with the butter and vinegar. Swirl the beets until evenly coated and creamy, being careful not to brown the butter. Season with pepper, remove from the heat and keep warm until needed.

When ready to serve

On a clean surface carve the lamb leg into thin slices and mound in the center of 4 warm dinner plates. Garnish with white cheddar grits and striped beets. Finish with a drizzle of huckleberry jelly.

lobster

corn dog | tasso spinach | ballpark mustard

This dish has, in one form or another, been one of my cover girls for over 10 years now. The presentation might look difficult but it shows your guest that you used a whole lobster and the wow factor is off the charts!

To build the dish
lobster
corn dog
tasso spinach
ballpark mustard

Serves 4

For the lobster

4 hard shell maritime lobsters about 1¾ lb (875 g) each
16 cups (4 L) court bouillon, boiling (recipe page 148)
¼ lb (125 g) sweet butter
2 Tbsp (30 mL) smoked Spanish paprika
coarse salt
freshly ground white pepper

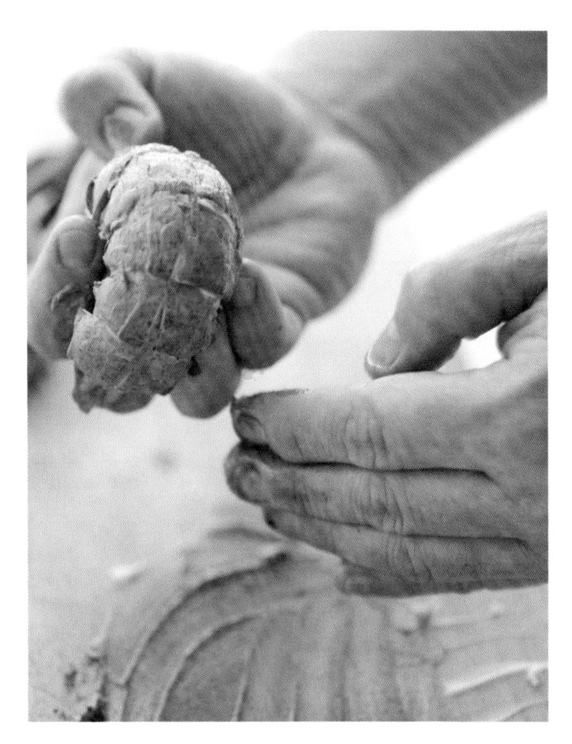

Preheat oven to 375°F (190°C). Place a wire rack over a sheet pan.

Carefully remove the rubber bands from the lobster claws. Blanch the lobsters in the boiling court bouillon for 3–4 minutes. Transfer to a sheet pan and let cool completely. Break the claws from the body, crack the shells and remove the meat. Cover and refrigerate the claw meat until you make the corn dogs. Twist the tails off the bodies—fold the tail fins back until you break them from the tail shell. Press the tail between your palms and crack the shell. Gently remove the tail meat and use a paring knife to butterfly the tail open and remove the intestinal track. Pull the head apart to expose the inside. Use your fingers to pull the soft lung flaps from the body and discard. Trim the bottom set of legs, rinse and reserve. Use kitchen shears to trim the head shell into an even-ended cylinder about 2 inches (5 cm) in height. Rinse in cold water and insert the legs portion into the cylinder. Refrigerate, covered, until needed. Use your fingers to blend the butter and paprika into a smooth paste. Gently rub into the tails and place to the side.

lobster (continued)

For the corn dog

3 oz (75 g) shrimp, peeled and deveined
¼ cup (60 mL) whipping (35%) cream
4 oz (100 g) claw meat, cut into ¼-inch (0.5-cm) dice
2 scallions, washed and minced
4–5 sprigs chervil, stems removed
coarse salt
freshly grated white pepper
4 cups (1 L) vegetable stock (recipe page 150)
1 cup (250 mL) instant tempura batter mix
½ cup (125 mL) cornmeal
1 bottle (341 mL) dark beer

In a small food processor fitted with a metal blade pulse the shrimp and cream until smooth, about 30 seconds. Remove and transfer to a large nonreactive bowl. Add the lobster meat, minced scallions and chervil leaves. Season with salt and pepper and refrigerate, covered, until cold, about 30 minutes.

Place a small piece of plastic wrap on a clean work surface and drop about ¼ cup (60 mL) of lobster mixture in the center. Bring the bottom of the plastic wrap up to meet the top end, press down around the mixture and roll, keeping the cylinder shape. Tie one end and use your fingers to squeeze out any remaining air bubbles while keeping the sausage shape intact. Tie the other end. Use a clean pushpin to poke 4–5 holes in the sausage.

Prepare a bowl of ice water.

Blanch the sausage in simmering stock until firm to the touch, about 3 minutes. Remove and shock in the ice water. When completely cold, snip the ends off the plastic wrap and carefully unwrap. Pat dry and place on paper towels in the refrigerator.

In a large nonreactive bowl mix the tempura and cornmeal with a whisk. Slowly add the beer until you have a smooth batter with no visible lumps. Let the batter rest about 10 minutes. If it's too thick just thin it down with a little more beer.

Preheat deep-fryer to 325°F (160°C).

Skewer the lobster sausages and dip in the batter, rolling the sausages to coat them evenly. Remove and carefully transfer to the deep-fryer. Cook until golden brown, about 2–3 minutes. Remove and transfer to paper towels. Keep warm until needed.

For the tasso spinach

½ lb (250 g) baby spinach, washed and spun dry
1 tsp (5 mL) olive oil
2 oz (50 g) tasso ham (or serrano ham), julienne
1 Tbsp (15 mL) sweet butter
coarse salt
freshly ground black pepper

In a large sauté pan over medium heat sweat the spinach in the olive oil until soft and bright green. Add the tasso ham and butter and mix well. Season to taste with salt and pepper. Remove from the heat and keep warm until needed.

For the ballpark mustard

2 Tbsp (30 mL) dried mustard powder
¼ cup (60 mL) Dijon mustard
3 Tbsp (45 mL) champagne vinegar
½ tsp (2 mL) turmeric powder
coarse salt as needed

In a small saucepan over low heat, bring all the ingredients to a simmer. Whisk until smooth and bright yellow. Adjust the seasoning with salt. Remove from the heat and let cool. Refrigerate, covered, until needed.

When ready to serve

Fill the bodies with tasso spinach and top with reserved tails. Transfer to the prepared sheet pan and bake until the tails are firm to the touch, about 5–7 minutes. Remove and place the lobster bodies in the center of 4 warm dinner plates. Rest a corn dog against the legs and garnish with ballpark mustard.

halibut

crab hash | angry fritters | saffron aioli

Halibut is one of those fish that can take on a wide range of flavors and still shine through. Crab is one of my personal favorite pairings for halibut.

To build the dish
halibut
crab hash
angry fritters
saffron aioli

Serves 4

For the halibut

28 oz (825 g) halibut, skin and pin bones removed
2 Tbsp (30 mL) olive oil
1 Tbsp (15 mL) pink peppercorns
1 chipotle pepper, stem and seeds removed
1 tsp (5 mL) coriander seeds, crushed
1 tsp (5 mL) black peppercorns, crushed
coarse salt

Preheat oven to 350°F (180°C).

Cut the halibut into 4 fillets, about 7 oz (200 g) each. Brush with the olive oil and reserve.

In a mortar and pestle, prepare a chipotle pepper dust by grinding the pink peppercorns, chipotle pepper, coriander seeds and black peppercorns until coarse. Remove and reserve until needed. In a large non-stick sauté pan over medium heat sear the halibut fillets on all sides until just starting to turn golden. Remove and transfer to a non-stick sheet pan. Sprinkle with the chipotle pepper dust and season with salt. Roast on the middle rack of the oven until firm to the touch, about 7–10 minutes. Rest in a warm place until needed.

For the crab hash

1 cup (250 mL) jumbo lump crab meat
1 ear peaches and cream corn, niblets removed
1 small yellow pepper, roasted, skinned and diced
2 scallions, washed and minced
1 Tbsp (15 mL) sweet butter
1 Tbsp (15 mL) extra virgin olive oil
1 lime, juice and zest
coarse salt

Preheat broiler to 500°F (260°C).

Spread the crab meat over a sheet pan and quickly place under the element, if any shell pieces remain they will pop and turn bright white. Remove and discard any shell pieces and place the meat in a large nonreactive bowl. In a small frying pan sweat the corn niblets, yellow pepper and scallion in the butter and olive oil until the corn turns translucent, about 4–5 minutes. Remove from the heat and let cool completely. Add crabmeat and season with lime juice, zest and salt and keep covered in the refrigerator until needed.

halibut (continued)

For the angry fritters

½ lb (250 g) jumbo lump crab meat crab, picked clean of all shells
2 scallions, washed and julienne
½ tsp (2 mL) saffron threads
1 Tbsp (15 mL) boiling water
1 jalapeño pepper, seeded and minced
½ cup (125 mL) tempura batter mix
2 Tbsp (30 mL) cornmeal
soda water, as needed
coarse salt
freshly ground black pepper
vegetable oil for deep-frying

Preheat deep-fryer to 375°F (190°C).

In a large nonreactive bowl add the crab and scallions. In a small cup steep the saffron in boiling water for 3 minutes. Add the saffron tea and jalapeño to the crab and scallions and mix until evenly incorporated. Add the tempura batter mix and cornmeal and mix gently until just incorporated. Slowly add the soda water until the dry ingredients just come together. You want a fairly thick and sticky mixture. Season with salt and pepper then carefully drop 1 Tbsp (15 mL) of batter at a time into the deep-fryer, flipping continuously until it's bright yellow. Remove from the fryer and drain on paper towel. Keep warm until needed.

For the saffron aioli

1 tsp (5 mL) saffron threads
2 Tbsp (30 mL) hot water
2 large egg yolks
2 garlic cloves, peeled and minced
4–5 drops Tabasco sauce
½ tsp (2 mL) coarse salt
1 Tbsp (15 mL) lemon juice
1 cup (250 mL) olive oil

Combine the saffron and hot water and steep for about 3 minutes. Combine the egg yolks, garlic, Tabasco, salt and lemon juice in a food processor fitted with a steel blade. Add the steeped saffron and water and blend for 30 seconds with the motor running. With the food processor running, slowly add the olive oil in a steady stream until an emulsion forms. Remove and refrigerate, covered, until needed.

When ready to serve

Spoon equal amounts of the saffron aioli in the center of 4 warm dinner plates and spread with a pallet knife. Mound some of the crab hash and place halibut on top. Garnish with angry fritters.

whole duck

five-spice glaze | scallion mu shu | buddha's vegetables

Don't be overwhelmed by the prospect of roasting a whole duck. It's really not that difficult. Use the roasting time to make the mu shu and do all your vegetable prep.

To build the dish
whole duck
five-spice glaze
scallion mu shu
buddha's vegetables

Serves 4

For the whole duck

- 2 ducks with heads on, washed, about 4–5 lb (2 kg) each
- 2 oranges, quartered
- 4 pieces star anise
- 4 sticks cinnamon
- 4 cloves garlic
- 1 Tbsp (15 mL) Szechuan peppercorns
- 1 Tbsp (15 mL) fennel seeds
- 8 cloves
- ½ cup (125 mL) rice wine vinegar
- 2 Tbsp (30 mL) pomegranate molasses

Preheat oven to 325°F (160°C).

Fill the ducks with the oranges and spices. Use a large metal skewer to stitch the belly flaps closed. Mix the vinegar and pomegranate molasses together in a small bowl and brush all over the ducks. Place the ducks in a heavy-bottomed roasting pan, transfer to the middle rack of the oven and roast for 30 minutes. Remove from the oven and pour off the accumulated fat. Flip the ducks over and return them to the oven. Repeat this process until the ducks are deep brown in color, about 90 minutes. Remove from the heat and prop up on the side of the roasting pan to help continue to drain the fat for about 15 minutes. Place each duck over a large bowl, remove the metal skewer, drain and reserve all the contents.

Preheat broiler. Place a wire rack over a sheet pan.

On a cutting board debone the breasts and trim each leg into 2 pieces, thigh and drumstick. Reserve the carcass for the sauce. Place duck meat on the prepared sheet pan and place under the broiler to crisp the skin, about 2 minutes. Remove and keep warm until needed.

For the five-spice glaze

- contents of duck cavities
- 1 tsp (5 mL) ginger, minced
- 1 tsp (5 mL) sesame oil
- 2 red plums, pits removed and chopped
- ½ cup (125 mL) plum wine
- duck carcasses, chopped
- 1 cup (250 mL) dark chicken stock (recipe page 148)

Pass the contents of the duck cavities through a fine mesh sieve. Save the liquid and discard the solids. In a small saucepan over medium heat sauté the ginger in the sesame oil until fragrant, about 30 seconds. Add the plums and continue to cook for another 5 minutes. Deglaze with plum wine and add the reserved liquid, duck carcasses and chicken stock. Bring to a boil, reduce the heat and simmer, uncovered, for 15 minutes. Remove from the heat and strain 2–3 times through a fine mesh sieve. Adjust the seasoning to taste if necessary. Remove from the heat and keep warm until needed.

For the scallion mu shu

- 1 bunch scallions, green parts only
- 1½ cups (375 mL) water
- 1½ cups (375 mL) all-purpose flour
- 4 large eggs
- 1 tsp (5 mL) coarse salt
- 1 Tbsp (15 mL) peanut oil

In a food processor fitted with a metal blade blend the scallion greens and water until smooth, about 30 seconds. Remove and pass through a fine mesh strainer. Quickly rinse and dry the bowl of the food processor and blend the flour, eggs, salt and scallion water until all the ingredients are thoroughly combined. Remove and let this batter rest for 10 minutes at room temperature. Dab a folded paper towel in the peanut oil and brush the bottom of a large non-stick pan over medium heat. Pour in about ¼ cup (60 mL) of batter and immediately swirl to coat the entire bottom of the pan. Cook the crêpe until golden brown, about 2–3 minutes. Flip and brown the other side, about 1 minute. Transfer to a clean kitchen towel and repeat with the remaining batter. Keep covered with a kitchen towel until ready to serve.

For the buddha's vegetables

- 4 oz (100 g) extra-firm tofu
- 1 Tbsp (15 mL) cornstarch
- 1 cup (250 mL) peanut oil, for frying
- ½ oz (12 g) white snow fungus
- 1 oz (25 g) dried elephant ear mushrooms
- 1 square fermented bean curd sheet
- 4 cups (1 L) boiling water for rehydrating
- 3 cloves garlic, peeled and minced
- 1 oz (25 g) ginger, peeled and minced
- 1 Tbsp (15 mL) sesame oil
- 2 oz (50 g) bamboo shoots
- 1 carrot, peeled and crinkle-cut into ¼-inch (0.5-cm) slices
- ¼ cup (60 mL) snow peas, stem and strings removed
- 8 Chinese long beans, cut into 3-inch (7.5-cm) lengths
- 3 scallions, trimmed and cut into 2-inch (5-cm) lengths
- 2 Tbsp (30 mL) vegetarian oyster sauce
- 1 Tbsp (15 mL) soy sauce
- 2 Tbsp (30 mL) Chinese rice wine

Gently press the tofu between two clean kitchen towels to remove any excess moisture. Cut into ½-inch (1-cm) dice and toss with the cornstarch until evenly coated. In a wok over high heat fry the dusted tofu cubes in the peanut oil until golden brown, about 2 minutes. Remove and drain on paper towels. In a large bowl soak the snow fungus, mushrooms and fermented bean curd in the boiling water until soft, about 10 minutes. Drain and reserve until needed. In a wok over high heat stir-fry the garlic and ginger in the sesame oil for 5 seconds. Add the vegetables and continue to stir-fry until mixed evenly. Add the tofu, fungus, mushrooms and bean curd and continue cooking. Deglaze with the oyster sauce, soy sauce and rice wine. Reduce until the vegetables are shiny and all the liquid has evaporated. Remove from the heat and keep warm until needed.

When ready to serve

Spoon some buddha's vegetables in the center of 4 warm dinner plates and place a duck breast, thigh and drumstick around them. Drizzle with five-spice glaze and garnish with a folded scallion mu shu and more buddha's vegetables.

west coast crab

pepper cress | pimento bisque | Old Bay madeleines

This is probably the most difficult soup bowl you'll ever have to make and you might think that you have too many madeleines but believe me, you'll need every last one of them to dip in the bisque.

To build the dish
west coast crab
pepper cress
pimento bisque
Old Bay madeleines

Serves 4

For the west coast crab

4 west coast crabs about 2 lb (1 kg) each
16 cups (4L) court bouillon
(recipe page 148)
2 Tbsp (30 mL) Old Bay seasoning
4 cups (1 L) pimento bisque

In a large stockpot over high heat bring the court bouillon to a boil. Add the Old Bay seasoning and the crabs. Cook for 6–7 minutes. Remove from the water and let cool completely.

Set the crab shell up, hold the legs down with one hand and pull off the top of the crab. Pull away and discard the gills from each side of the crab. Pull off and discard the mouth section. Turn the crab over, revealing the tail. Twist off and discard. Snap off the legs where they join the body. Wash the top shell, legs and body under cold water, removing any debris. Crack the claws with a rolling pin and carefully remove as much meat as possible. Use kitchen shears to snip the body into smaller pieces, making it easer to remove the meat. Repeat for each crab. Reserve the top shell and all the meat.

For the pepper cress

2 bunches pepper cress, washed and larger stems removed
2 Tbsp (30 mL) olive oil
½ Tbsp (7 mL) lemon juice
½ cup (125 mL) sherry vinegar
1 very ripe avocado, peeled and diced
coarse salt
freshly ground black pepper

In a large nonreactive bowl mix the pepper cress with the olive oil, lemon juice and sherry vinegar until evenly coated. Add the avocado and season to taste with salt and pepper. Reserve until needed.

For the pimento bisque

1 lb (500 g) black tiger shrimp, 16–20 count, butterflied with the shell on, intestinal track removed
¼ cup (60 mL) olive oil
1 small onion, peeled and thinly sliced
2 ribs celery, peeled and thinly sliced
2 medium carrots, peeled and thinly sliced
3 cloves garlic, peeled and sliced
¼ cup (60 mL) brandy
6 Roma tomatoes, cored and sliced
1 Tbsp (15 mL) tomato paste
½ cup (125 mL) piquillo peppers
¼ cup (60 mL) long-grain rice
1 cup (250 mL) shellfish stock
(recipe page 149)
cayenne pepper
coarse salt

In a large saucepan over high heat sauté the shrimp in the olive oil until the shells turn bright pink, about 2 minutes. Use tongs to pick out the shrimps and let cool enough to touch. Add the onion, celery, carrots and garlic and continue to cook until the onion turns translucent, about 4–5 minutes.

Remove the pan from the heat and add the brandy, bringing it slowly back over the heat until it ignites. When the flame burns out add the tomatoes, tomato paste and piquillo peppers and continue to cook until the tomatoes start to disintegrate, about 7–10 minutes. Add the rice and stock and bring to a boil. Reduce the heat and simmer, uncovered, until the rice is tender, about 20 minutes. Peel the shrimp, chop the meat into small dice and return to the sauce. Remove from the heat and cool slightly, about 5 minutes. Purée in a food processor fitted with a metal blade until smooth. Pass through a fine mesh strainer, adjust the seasoning with salt and pepper and keep warm until needed.

For the Old Bay madeleines

- 4 whole eggs
- 2 cups (500 mL) granulated sugar
- 2 cups (500 mL) all-purpose flour
- 1 ½ cups (375 mL) clarified butter
- 1 Tbsp (15 mL) sherry
- 1 tsp (5 mL) Old Bay seasoning

Preheat oven to 425°F (220°C). Coat 2 non-stick 18-cup madeleine molds with vegetable spray then dust with flour.

In the top of a double boiler stir the eggs and sugar until creamy and warm to the touch. Remove from the heat and beat until cool, about 5 minutes. Add the flour gradually, mixing well. Add the butter, sherry and Old Bay seasoning and mix until incorporated. Drop the batter into the prepared madeleine molds and bake until light golden brown, about 10 minutes. Remove and turn out onto a clean kitchen towel. Keep warm until needed.

When ready to serve

Heat the pimento bisque with the reserved crab meat and ladle into the reserved crab shell tops and place in the center of 4 warm dinner bowls. Garnish with pepper cress and Old Bay madeleines.

arctic char

fennel braise | icicle radish | Yukon gold dumplings

Arctic char is more closely related to the trout than to the salmon. While char can grow up to 25 lb (11 kg) in the wild you will find most farmed fish weigh in at about 4–5 lb (around 2 kg).

To build the dish
Arctic char
fennel braise
icicle radish
Yukon gold dumplings

Serves 4

For the Arctic char

4 Arctic char steaks about ½ lb (250 g) each
4 scallions, blanched and shocked, cut into ribbons
2 Tbsp (30 mL) sweet butter, melted
coarse salt
freshly ground white pepper
4 oz (100 g) char or trout caviar

Preheat oven to 375°F (190°C). Line a sheet pan with parchment paper.

Pull any visible pin bones from the steaks. Fold the belly flaps under to form a circle and tie with a scallion ribbon. Brush with butter and season with salt and pepper. Place on the prepared sheet pan and roast until firm to the touch, about 7–8 minutes.

Remove from the heat and keep warm until needed. Reserve the caviar until ready to plate.

For the fennel braise

2 large heads fennel
1 Tbsp (15 mL) sweet butter
coarse salt
freshly ground white pepper
4 cups (1 L) vegetable stock (recipe page 150)

Preheat oven to 325°F (160°C).

Trim the fronds off the fennel and reserve. Cut the bulbs in half and remove the core. Use a Japanese mandoline to cut it into ribbons ⅛ inch (3 mm) thick. In a small saucepan over medium heat sweat the fennel ribbons in the butter until soft, about 5 minutes. Season with salt and pepper and cover with the stock. Bring to a boil and remove from the heat. Cover and transfer to the middle rack of the oven. Braise until very soft, about 30 minutes. Remove from the heat and keep warm until needed.

For the icicle radish

½ lb (250 g) icicle radishes
1 Tbsp (15 mL) sweet butter
coarse salt

Trim the tops of the radishes and wash gently under cold water. In a small saucepan of boiling water blanch the radishes until soft to the touch, about 2–3 minutes. Drain and toss with the butter and salt. Keep warm until needed.

For the Yukon gold dumplings

- 2 large Yukon gold potatoes, scrubbed
- ⅓ cup (75 mL) finely grated Parmesan cheese
- 1 large egg
- 2 Tbsp (30 mL) coarse salt
- freshly grated white pepper
- 1 cup (250 mL) all-purpose flour
- butter to coat the dumplings

Line a sheet pan with parchment paper.

In a small stockpot cover the potatoes with water, add 1 Tbsp (15 mL) of the salt and bring to a boil. Cook until they slip off the tip of a paring knife. Drain and peel the potatoes as soon as you can handle them. Pass through a potato ricer onto the prepared sheet pan in an even layer. Try not to over-handle. Transfer to the refrigerator to cool, about 15 minutes. Place the cooled purée on a clean work surface, create a mound with a well in the center and add the remaining ingredients. Mix as gently as possible until a rough dough forms. Lightly dust with more flour and continue to knead until a smooth dough forms. Use your hands to pat the dough into a rectangle and cut into 1-inch (2.5-cm) strips. Cut these into 1-inch (2.5-cm) squares and make a gentle pinch in the center. Bring a large pot of water to a boil and add the remaining salt and the dumplings. Cook until they float then remove with a slotted spoon. Transfer to a bowl with butter, toss to evenly coat and keep warm until needed.

When ready to serve

Place the char in the center of 4 warm dinner plates and top with caviar. Spoon individual piles of the fennel braise, icicle radish and Yukon gold dumplings to the side.

Warm

March | April | May

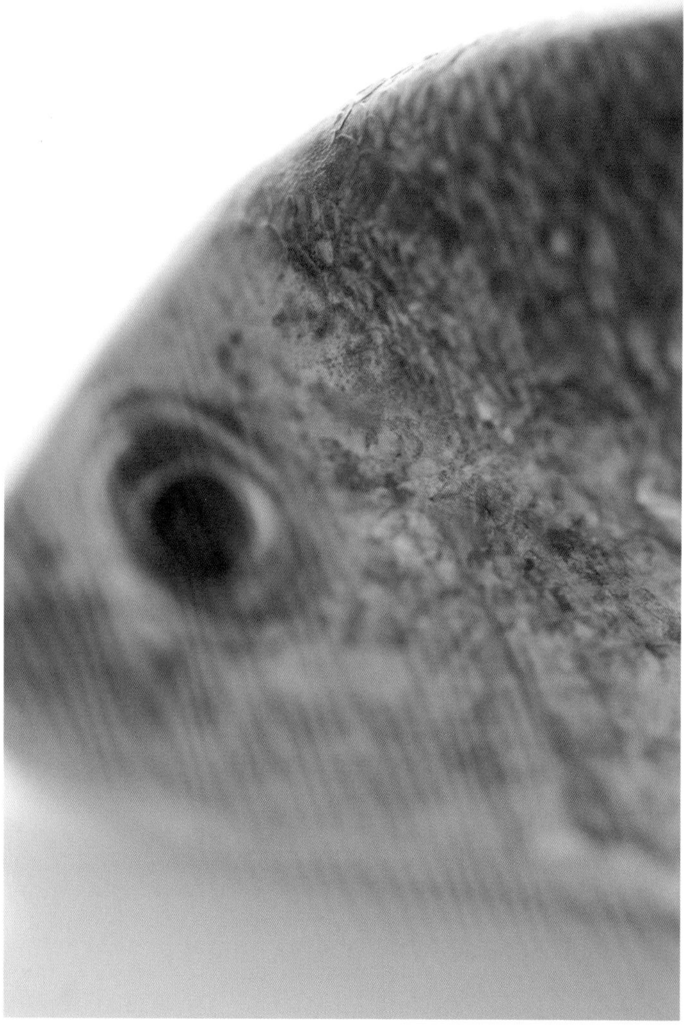

When I'm Warm

March | April | May

The only reason why I love going to the market is meeting other people who are as crazy about food as I am. Gramercy Market in New York is just one of my favorites.

I was living in New York, running a major hotel (now run by the devil himself, Chef Gordon Ramsay) and still commuting from Toronto every week. "Me-time" was exceptionally rare. However, I could justify taking a walk outside if a market was involved and I had a few staff in tow to carry my chosen food-finds back to the hotel. There, I would create something special for our guests and stretch out the creativity inside me, above and beyond our menus in the hotel.

New York has places like Chinatown, Motts Street and some of the best green markets around. You'd be surprised at how many menus in New York City's fine restaurants are created from scratch thanks to these markets. Sometimes, it only takes a farmer with passion for his purple potatoes to get your creative juices flowing.

veal chop

arugula | Parmesan mushrooms | cipolline onions

When breaded veal is ordered, the cut is usually not obvious. I prefer to leave the bone in for this dish to show my dinner guests I'm only using the best cut of meat.

To build the dish
veal chops
Parmesan mushrooms
cipolline onions
arugula

Serves 4

For the veal chops

- 4 naturally farmed veal chops, about 16 oz each (450 g)
- 1 cup (250 mL) all-purpose flour
- coarse salt
- freshly ground black pepper
- 3 eggs, lightly beaten
- 2 cups (500 mL) fresh breadcrumbs
- ½ cup (125 mL) freshly grated Parmesan cheese
- ¼ cup (60 mL) sweet butter
- ¼ cup (60 mL) olive oil

Place the veal chops between 2 pieces of plastic wrap. Holding on to the bone firmly, pound the veal with the smooth side of a meat tenderizer until even and about ¼ inch (0.5 cm) thick. Place the flour in a shallow baking dish and season with salt and pepper. Put the beaten eggs in another dish and season with salt and pepper. Combine the breadcrumbs and Parmesan cheese in a third dish and season with salt and pepper. Holding the rib bone, follow the standard breading procedure with the veal. Continue until all the veal chops are breaded. Keep the breaded chops on a parchment paper-lined sheet pan sprinkled with a little breadcrumb mix.

Preheat oven to 375°F (190°C). Place a wire rack on a sheet pan.

In an extra-large frying pan over medium heat add 1 Tbsp (15 mL) of the butter and 1 Tbsp (15 mL) of the olive oil. When the butter starts to bubble carefully add 1 veal chop and sauté until golden brown, about 3–4 minutes. Flip and continue to cook on the other side until golden brown. Remove from the pan and transfer to the prepared sheet pan. Quickly wipe the frying pan with a kitchen towel and repeat until all the chops have been sautéed. Transfer to the middle rack of the oven and cook until there is no sign of blood directly around the bone, about 4–5 minutes. Remove and keep in a warm place.

For the Parmesan mushrooms

½ lb (225 g) oyster mushrooms
1 shallot, peeled and sliced thinly
2 Tbsp (30 mL) olive oil
4–5 cloves roasted garlic, smashed
coarse salt
freshly ground black pepper
½ cup (125 mL) Parmesan cheese

Preheat oven to 475°F (240°C).

Brush the bases of the oyster mushrooms to remove any dirt. In a large frying pan over medium heat sauté the shallot in olive oil until translucent, about 2 minutes. Add the roasted garlic and mushrooms. Continue to cook until the mushrooms just begin to soften, about 3 minutes. Remove from the heat and arrange in 4 little piles on an unlined sheet pan. Sprinkle with Parmesan cheese and transfer to the middle rack of the oven. Bake until the cheese turns a light brown, about 3–4 minutes. Remove from the heat and keep warm until needed.

For the cipolline onions

12 oz (350 g) cipolline onions
2 Tbsp (30 mL) olive oil
coarse salt
freshly ground black pepper

Preheat oven to 325°F (160°C).

Toss the onions with the olive oil in a stainless steel bowl until well coated. Season with salt and pepper and place on a sheet pan. Transfer to the middle rack of the oven and roast until the onions are soft to the touch, about 30 minutes. Remove and let cool until the onions can be handled comfortably. Carefully peel the onions, keeping their shape and integrity. Reserve in a warm place.

For the arugula

4 cups (1 L) spring arugula
3 Tbsp (45 mL) extra virgin olive oil
½ lemon, juice only
1 Tbsp (15 mL) white balsamic vinegar
coarse salt
freshly ground black pepper

In a large nonreactive bowl toss the arugula with the olive oil, lemon juice and vinegar. Mix together until just coated. Season with salt and pepper and serve immediately.

When ready to serve

Place a veal chop in the center of 4 warm dinner plates and top with some of the Parmesan mushrooms and cipolline onions. Serve the arugula on the side.

lamb loin

grape leaves | Greek salad | oregano smashed potatoes

I love souvlaki so much that I created this dressed-up version. Whenever I use grape leaves in a dish, you know I'm having fun in the kitchen.

To build the dish
lamb loins
Greek salad
oregano smashed potatoes

Serves 4

For the lamb loins

4 lamb loins, to a total weight of 1½ lb (750 g), silver skin removed
1 Tbsp (15 mL) olive oil
coarse salt as needed
freshly ground black pepper
8–10 grape leaves in brine, depending on size
¼ cup (60 mL) sun-dried tomato spread (recipe page 151)

Preheat oven to 375°F (190°C). Place a wire rack on a sheet pan.

Coat the lamb loins with the olive oil, and season with salt and pepper. In a large frying pan over high heat sear the lamb loins until well caramelized on all sides, about 4–5 minutes. Remove from the heat and let cool enough to touch. Place 2 large grape leaves on a clean work surface and place a lamb loin in the center of each leaf. Top with 1 Tbsp (15 mL) of sun-dried tomato spread and spread from end to end. Fold the sides over and bring the bottom up. Roll with a little bit of tension until you have a snug log about 1 x 4 inches (2.5 x 10 cm). Continue until all 4 loins are wrapped. Transfer to the prepared sheet pan and roast until just firm to the touch, about 7 minutes. Remove from the heat and rest in a warm place.

For the Greek salad

1 yellow pepper, stem and seeds removed
1 red onion, peeled
1 hothouse cucumber, peeled and seeded
3 Tbsp (45 mL) extra virgin olive oil
1 Tbsp (15 mL) red wine vinegar
1 lemon, juice and zest
2 sprigs oregano, stems discarded
coarse salt
freshly ground black pepper
¼ cup (60 mL) black olive spread (recipe page 151)
2 oz (50 g) feta cheese, frozen

Dice the pepper, onion and cucumber as finely as possible and transfer to a large nonreactive bowl. Add the olive oil, red wine vinegar and lemon juice and zest. Stir until well coated. Add the oregano leaves, season with salt and pepper and mix until all the ingredients are blended. Let stand at room temperature until ready to serve.

For the oregano smashed potatoes

- 1 lb (500 g) marble-sized red-skinned potatoes, washed and scrubbed
- 2 Tbsp (30 mL) olive oil
- 1 lemon, zest only
- 12 cloves garlic, roasted
- 3–4 sprigs oregano, stems discarded
- coarse salt
- freshly ground black pepper

Place the potatoes in a large stockpot filled with water and bring to a boil over high heat. Cook until the potatoes slip off the tip of a small paring knife, about 12-15 minutes. Remove from the heat and drain. In a large saucepan over medium heat, place the potatoes, olive oil, lemon zest and roasted garlic. Sauté and gently mash the potatoes with the back of a wooden spoon. Add the oregano and season with salt and pepper. Remove from the heat and keep warm until needed.

When ready to serve

Spoon 1 Tbsp (15 mL) of black olive spread in the center of each of the 4 warm dinner plates then top with 2 Tbsp (30 mL) of Greek salad. Grate the frozen feta cheese overtop. On a clean work surface cut the lamb loins in half and place on top of the salad. Garnish with the oregano smashed potatoes.

grouper

yellow pepper | purple potato | pink grapefruit

The banana leaf is the real trick to this dish. You have to try it once, just to really experience the tropical feel of grouper wrapped in its own serving vessel. It's easier than it looks and banana leaves are unexpectedly easy to find—just ask at any Latin market. The leaves are normally kept in frozen packages in the market and they thaw out perfectly! Banana leaves are wonderfully versatile. I use them to decorate plates when displaying food, appetizers and one-bites.

To build the dish
grouper
yellow pepper salad
purple potato salad
pink grapefruit salad
pink peppercorn vinaigrette

Serves 4

For the grouper

2 lb (1 kg) grouper fillets, skin and all bones removed
1 package banana leaves
1 lemon, sliced as thinly as possible
1 lime, sliced as thinly as possible
8 allspice berries
8 sprigs cilantro
8 sprigs thyme
4 sprigs dill
¼ cup (60 mL) olive oil
coarse salt
freshly ground black pepper

Preheat oven to 450°F (230°C). Place a wire rack on a sheet pan.

Slice the grouper into four 8-oz (250-g) portions. If you need to use a couple of smaller pieces to make up the weight, that's fine. Cut each banana leaf into a 12- x 12-inch (30- x 30-cm) square and place it flat. In the center of the banana leaf place a few slices of lemon and lime. To this add 2 allspice berries, 2 sprigs cilantro, 2 sprigs thyme and 1 sprig dill. Place the grouper on top and season with olive oil, salt and pepper. Fold the bottom and top of the banana leaf together and pinch one end. Tie with a scrap piece of banana leaf or string. From the open end push the grouper tight against the tied end. Pinch and tie the remaining end to close. Repeat with the remaining portions. Transfer to the prepared sheet pan and roast on the middle rack of the oven until firm to the touch, about 10–12 minutes. Remove from the heat, rest for 3–4 minutes and serve.

For the yellow pepper salad

1 yellow pepper
1 poblano pepper
1 sweet potato, peeled and cut into ¼-inch (0.5-cm) dice
1 cob corn, niblets removed
1 jalapeño pepper, split, seeded and minced
coarse salt
3 Tbsp (45 mL) pink peppercorn vinaigrette

Using a kitchen torch, carefully char off the skin of the yellow pepper. Wipe the black skin off with paper towels and cut in half. Discard the stem and seeds. Cut into ¼-inch (0.5-cm) dice and transfer to a non-reactive bowl. Repeat with the poblano pepper and add to the bowl.

In a small saucepan over low heat sauté the diced sweet potato until soft and lightly colored. Add the corn niblets and continue to cook until the corn has turned bright yellow. Remove from the heat and transfer to the bowl with the yellow and poblano peppers. Season with jalapeño, salt and vinaigrette. Keep covered at room temperature until needed.

grouper (continued)

For the purple potato salad

1 lb (500 g) purple potatoes
coarse salt as needed
2 Tbsp (30 mL) pink peppercorn vinaigrette

Peel the potatoes and cut into 1/4-inch (0.5-cm) slices. Place them in a small saucepan and cover with cold water. Gently simmer until the potatoes slip off the tip of a knife. Remove from the water, drain and cool completely. Transfer to a nonreactive bowl and season with salt and pink peppercorn vinaigrette. Keep covered at room temperature until needed.

For the pink grapefruit salad

2 pink grapefruits
7 1/2 oz (213 mL) can of hearts of palm
1 scallion, julienne
1 passion fruit, juice only
coarse salt
2 Tbsp (30 mL) pink peppercorn vinaigrette

Peel and section the grapefruits and place in a large nonreactive bowl. Cut the hearts of palm into 1/4-inch (0.5-cm) rounds and place in the bowl. Add the scallion and passion fruit juice and toss gently. Season with salt and vinaigrette. Keep covered at room temperature until needed.

For the pink peppercorn vinaigrette

1/2 cup (125 mL) extra virgin olive oil
2 tablespoons (30 mL) sherry vinegar
1 lime, juice only
2 tablespoons (30 mL) pink peppercorns
course salt

In a large nonreactive bowl, whisk all ingredients together until blended. Remove and store in a airtight container for up to 1 week.

When ready to serve

Place 3 equal mounds of each of the 3 salads on 4 rectangular warm dinner plates and garnish with the banana leaf grouper.

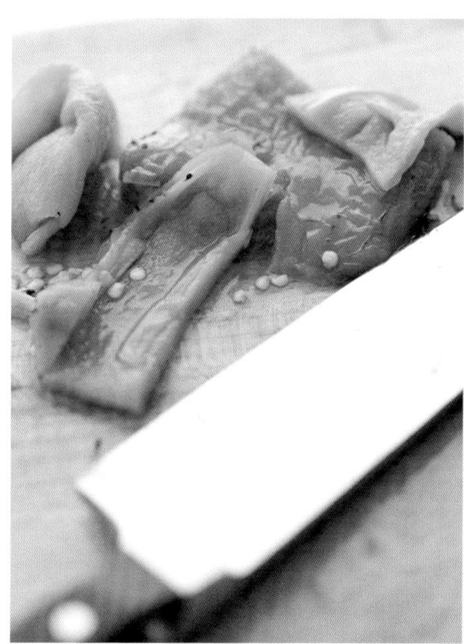

swordfish

annatto seed | pineapple | plantain chips

This fish is notorious for being served overcooked in many restaurants. Overcooking gives it a mealy, almost sawdust-like, texture. The idea behind this dish is to work with a thin cut and cook at a high, fast heat, searing in the juice and moisture of the fish.

To build the dish
swordfish
annatto seed rub
pineapple salsa
plantain chips

Serves 4

For the swordfish

- 2 lb (1 kg) center-cut swordfish
- ½ cup (125 mL) annatto seed rub
- coarse salt

Slice the swordfish into 8 pieces, about ¼ inch (0.5 cm) thick. Use your hands to rub the annatto seed rub into the swordfish and season lightly with salt. In a large cast iron frying pan over high heat sear the swordfish until a light char appears, about 30 seconds per side. Remove from the heat and keep warm until needed.

For the annatto seed rub

- ¼ cup (60 mL) achiote paste
- 4 limes, juice only
- ½ cup (125 mL) corn oil
- coarse salt

Place all the ingredients in a stainless steel bowl and mix with a wire whisk until smooth. Cover and refrigerate until needed.

For the pineapple salsa

- ½ pineapple, peeled
- ¼ cup (60 mL) corn oil
- 4 scallions, washed and roots removed
- 1 jalapeño pepper, stem and seeds removed
- 5–6 sprigs cilantro, washed and stems removed
- 2 limes, juice and zest
- coarse salt
- freshly ground black pepper

Slice the pineapple into ¼-inch (0.5-cm) slices. Use your hands to gently rub the slices with 1 tsp (5 mL) of the corn oil and char or grill in a hot pan until soft to the touch, about 1 minute per side. Remove from the heat and cut into ¼-inch (0.5-cm) dice. Place in a large nonreactive bowl. Mince the scallions and jalapeño and add to the bowl. Add the remaining corn oil, cilantro and lime juice and zest. Season with salt and pepper and keep covered room temperature until needed.

swordfish (continued)

For the plantain chips

- 2–3 green plantains
- vegetable oil for frying
- coarse salt

Preheat deep-fryer to 375°F (190°C).

With a paring knife, trim the top and bottom of the plantain. Use your finger to carefully peel the skin away from the plantain. Slice on the thinnest setting on a Japanese mandoline. Drop the plantain slices one by one into the deep-fryer and cook until crisp and bright yellow in color, about 2 minutes. Remove and transfer onto paper towels. Season with salt. Keep warm until needed.

When ready to serve

Place a slice of swordfish in the center of 4 warm dinner plates. Spoon some of the pineapple salsa and place another piece of swordfish on top. Garnish with plantain chips.

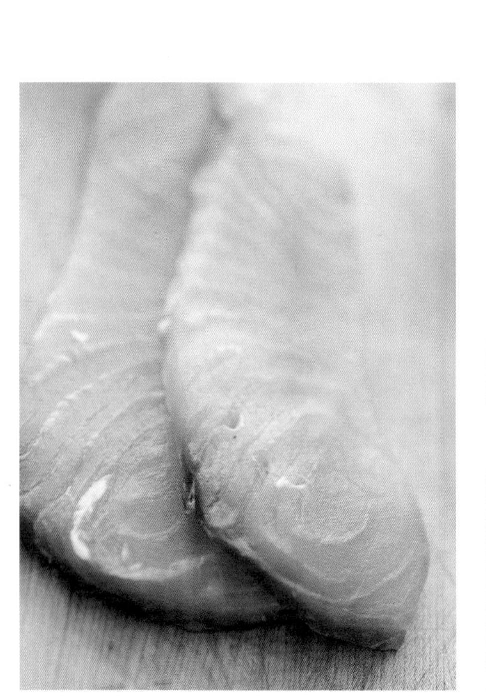

striped bass

olive tortellini | basil | tomato confit

I fell in love with this fish when I was living in California. I had spent the previous year working in Italy and this dish is the ultimate blending of two very distinct cultural experiences.

To build the dish
striped bass
lemon rub
olive tortellini
basil
tomato confit

Serves 4

For the striped bass

2 lb (1 kg) striped bass fillets, scales removed
1 Tbsp (15 mL) olive oil
2 Tbsp (30 mL) lemon rub
coarse salt

Place the striped bass skin side down on a clean work surface. Run your knife down the center of the fillet, from head to tail. Flip the fillets over and score the skin in a cross-hatched pattern in ½-inch (1-cm) intervals. Brush with olive oil and sear, skin side down, in a nonstick pan over medium-high heat. Sauté until the skin is crispy and golden brown, about 2 minutes. Flip and remove the pan from the heat. The carry-over heat in the pan should finish cooking the fish. Rest the fillets for 3–4 minutes before serving.

For the lemon rub

6 lemons, zest only
2 cloves garlic, peeled
4 sprigs thyme, stems removed
2 scallions, washed and chopped
¼ cup (60 mL) olive oil

In a food processor fitted with a metal blade pulse all the ingredients into a smooth paste. Keep covered in the refrigerator until needed.

For the olive tortellini

1¼ cups (310 mL) unbleached flour, plus additional for dusting the pasta dough
1¼ cups (310 mL) semolina flour
4 large eggs
1 tsp (5 mL) olive oil
2 Tbsp (30 mL) water
6 oz (150 g) cured black olives, pits removed
½ cup (125 mL) Parmesan cheese, grated
¼ cup (60 mL) sun-dried tomatoes
2 Tbsp (30 mL) olive oil
2 sprigs flat-leaf parsley, stems removed and chopped
1 clove garlic, peeled and minced
1 lemon, zest only
2 Tbsp (30 mL) sweet butter
coarse salt
freshly ground black pepper

In a food processor fitted with a metal blade, pulse the flours for 30 seconds to combine. Whisk the eggs and the 1 tsp (5 mL) of olive oil together in a small bowl. With the machine running, pour the egg mixture through the feed tube then add water just until the dough comes together into a mass, about 45 seconds. Check the consistency of the dough and adjust if needed. Process the dough for another 45 seconds and transfer to a lightly floured work surface. Knead the dough until smooth and resilient, about 7–10 minutes. Wrap the dough in plastic wrap.

Set the rollers on a pasta machine to their widest setting and place a bowl of flour nearby. Cut the dough into 4 equal portions and work with 1 portion at a time. Pat the dough to form a thick oblong, and run it through the machine. Fold the dough into thirds and repeat until the dough has straight, even sides about the width of the rollers. Dust with flour as needed. Continue to roll, reducing the width of the rollers until the dough has passed through the second-to-last setting and is about 1/16-inch (1.5 mm) thick. Lay the pasta sheets on a lightly floured work surface. Repeat the procedure with the remaining dough.

Dust a sheet pan with flour.

In a food processor fitted with a metal blade pulse the olives, Parmesan, sun-dried tomatoes, 2 Tbsp (30 mL) olive oil, parsley, garlic, zest and butter until smooth, about 45 seconds. Season to taste with salt and pepper. Remove and keep covered at room temperature until needed.

Use a 2-inch (5-cm) cutter to stamp out as many circles as you can from half the pasta. Loosely cover the other half with plastic wrap to prevent it from drying out. Drop about 1/2 tsp (2.5 mL) of filling in the center of each round. Fold the dough over to make a semicircle. Firmly press the edges to seal them, taking care to press out any air that may be trapped inside. Bring the pointed ends of each semicircle toward you. The cut edge of the semicircle should naturally fold up. Slightly overlap the ends and pinch to seal. Put on the prepared sheet pan. Continue with the rest of the pasta and filling.

Cook the tortellini in a large pot of boiling, salted water until just done, about 7 minutes.

Drain and toss with butter. Keep warm until needed.

For the basil

4 cups (1 L) basil leaves
canola oil, for deep-frying
coarse salt

Preheat deep-fryer to 375°F (190°C).

Wash and drain the basil leaves 4–5 times to remove all the sand. Transfer to a salad spinner and spin until completely dry. Sprinkle into the deep-fryer and cook until translucent green and crisp. Remove with a wire strainer and drain on paper towels. Season with salt and keep warm until needed.

For the tomato confit

16 Roma tomatoes
2 cups (500 mL) olive oil
1 Tbsp (15 mL) coriander seeds
1 tsp (5 mL) fennel seeds
4–5 cloves garlic, peeled and smashed
2–3 sprigs thyme
coarse salt
freshly ground black pepper

Preheat oven to 350°F (190°C). Prepare a bowl of ice water.

Using a paring knife score the tomatoes with a small cross on the bottom. Gently remove the core and plunge into boiling water for 15 seconds. Remove and transfer to the ice water to stop the cooking process. Carefully remove the skin and discard.

Place the tomatoes and the remaining ingredients in a small ovenproof baking dish. Transfer to the middle rack of the oven and bake for 25 minutes. Remove the from heat, discard the garlic and thyme and keep warm until needed.

When ready to serve

Spoon some of the tomato confit and an equal amount of the tortellini in the center of 4 warm dinner bowls. Place a striped bass fillet on top and garnish with crispy basil leaves.

lamb rack

parsley root spaetzle | squash | sun-dried cherry sauce

Chefs are often asked to create a new visual display on a classic style of meat. For example, lamb rack. The simple use of an acorn squash with stripes is used here as the supportive frame for the rack of lamb. This dish looks gorgeous on a plate and won't fail to impress your guests. I promise!

To build the dish
lamb rack
squash
spring vegetables
sun-dried cherry sauce
parsley root spaetzle

Serves 4

For the lamb rack

2 racks of lamb, about 20 oz (600 g) each
coarse salt
freshly ground black pepper
2 Tbsp (30 mL) olive oil

Preheat oven to 350°F (180°C). Place a wire rack over a sheet pan.

Trim the meat between the rib bones and cut the racks in half. Season with salt and pepper then drizzle with olive oil. In a large cast iron frying pan sear the lamb racks on all sides until golden brown, about 8–10 minutes. Remove from the heat, transfer to the prepared sheet pan and roast on the middle rack until the desired doneness is reached, about 12–15 minutes Remove from the heat and rest in a warm place until needed.

For the squash

2 small acorn squash
2 Tbsp (30 mL) sweet butter, melted
1 tsp (5 mL) brown sugar
2 sticks cinnamon, crushed
2 pieces star anise, crushed
4 pods green cardamom, crushed
4 cloves, crushed
coarse salt
freshly ground white pepper

Preheat oven to 325°F (160°C).

Use a vegetable peeler to stripe the acorn squashes on their raised ridges. Trim the top and bottom and cut in half. Use a spoon to remove all the seeds from the center of the rings.

Place the squash rings in an ovenproof baking dish. Brush with the melted butter and sprinkle with brown sugar. Distribute the crushed spices equally in the center of each squash ring. Season with salt and pepper, cover and bake until bright yellow and soft to the touch, about 20 minutes. Remove and keep warm until needed.

For the spring vegetables

¾ lb (375 g) assorted spring vegetables (carrots, haricots verts, green and white asparagus, etc.)
2 Tbsp (30 mL) sweet butter
coarse salt

Prepare a bowl of ice water.

Wash and trim the vegetables then blanch them all separately in a large pot of boiling salted water and shock in ice water. Drain and warm in a small saucepan over low heat with butter and salt. Keep warm until needed.

lamb rack (continued)

For the sun-dried cherry sauce

1 Tbsp (15 mL) granulated sugar
2 Tbsp (30 mL) raspberry vinegar
½ cup (125 mL) cognac
2 cups (500 mL) veal demi-glace (recipe page 150)
½ cup (125 mL) sun-dried cherries
1 orange, zest only

In a small saucepan over medium heat melt the sugar until light amber, about 2–3 minutes. Stop the browning by removing from the heat and adding the vinegar. Return to the heat and deglaze with the cognac. Add the demi-glace, cherries and orange zest. Cook to reduce slightly, about 15 minutes. Adjust the sweet-sour balance according to taste. Remove from the heat and keep warm until needed.

For the parsley root spaetzle

2–3 parsley roots, peeled and chopped
3 cups (750 mL) all-purpose flour
1 tsp (5 mL) salt
6 large eggs
2 Tbsp (30 mL) sweet butter
coarse salt
freshly ground black pepper

In a small saucepan over medium heat bring the parsnips to a boil in enough water to cover completely. Cook until the parsnips begin to disintegrate, about 15 minutes. Remove from the heat and let cool slightly. Blend the parsnips and 1 cup (250 mL) of the cooking liquid in a food processor fitted with a metal blade until smooth. Remove, cool and reserve.

In a large mixing bowl, combine the flour and salt and make a well in the center. In a small mixing bowl, whisk the egg and parsley root purée together and pour into the well. Use a wooden spoon to begin stirring the mixture, incorporating a little flour each time you stir, until you have a thick, wet, doughy mixture. Continue working the dough, lifting it up as you stir to incorporate as much air as possible. It should be thick enough to cling to the spoon then drop off.

Transfer the spaetzle mix to a plastic squeeze bottle and drop in batches into salted boiling water. When the spaetzle rise to the surface, give them a gentle stir and cook for about 20 seconds. Drain in a colander before tossing with butter, salt and pepper. Serve immediately.

When ready to serve

Place a squash ring in the center of 4 warm dinner plates and fill it with equal amounts of parsley root spaetzle and spring vegetables. On a clean work surface carve the lamb racks into 4 double-cut chops and place 2 chops on each filled squash ring. Finish with sun-dried cherry sauce.

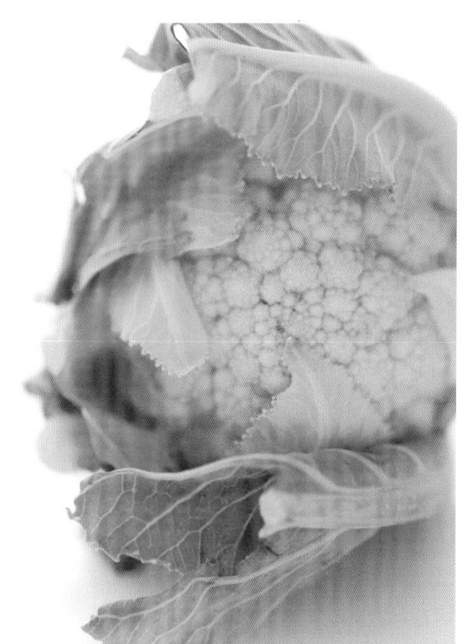

trout

potato salad | white asparagus | lobster 3

As you can tell, trout works exceptionally well with the taste of lobster. The fingers are another of my cover-girl dishes!

To build the dish

trout
potato salad
white asparagus
lobster compound butter
lobster sauce
lobster fingers

Serves 4

For the trout

4 whole trout, about 12 oz (350 g) each
1 Tbsp (15 mL) grape seed oil
coarse salt

Preheat oven to 400°F (200°C). Line a sheet pan with parchment paper.

Remove both fillets from each trout and use fishbone tweezers to remove the tiny pin bones from the middle of the fillets. Gently rub your index finger up and down the fillet to see if you've left any bones. Brush the fillets with the oil and season with salt. Transfer to the prepared sheet pan and top each fillet with a slice of lobster compound butter. Bake until the flesh is firm to the touch, about 5 minutes. Remove from the heat, and keep warm.

For the potato salad

1 lb (500 g) fingerling potatoes
4 slices smoky bacon, julienne
1 dill pickle, minced
1 red onion, peeled and minced
2 Tbsp (30 mL) Creole mustard
1 Tbsp (15 mL) storebought mayonnaise
1 tsp (5 mL) honey
½ cup (125 mL) dill fronds, loosely packed
coarse salt

Submerge the potatoes in cold water in a medium stockpot. Bring to a boil and cook until the potatoes slip off the end of a paring knife, about 10–12 minutes, depending on the size of the potatoes. Remove from the heat and drain. Cool until you can handle them comfortably and slice into ¼-inch (0.5-cm) rounds. Place in a large bowl and reserve.

In a small frying pan over low heat sauté the bacon until just crisp, about 15 minutes. Remove from the heat and drain off any excess fat. Pour the bacon over the sliced potatoes, add the minced pickle and red onion and mix with a wooden spoon. Add the mustard, mayonnaise and honey and mix gently to incorporate. Add the dill fronds and season with salt and pepper. Keep covered at room temperature until ready to serve.

trout (continued)

For the white asparagus

- 1 lb (500 g) white asparagus
- 2 cups (500 mL) whole milk
- 2 cups (500 mL) vegetable stock (recipe page 150)
- 2 Tbsp (30 mL) sweet butter
- coarse salt

Holding the tip of the asparagus with your fingers gently peel down the stalk. Rotate the spear and continue until all the skin has been removed. Trim into 3-inch (7.5-cm) spears, transfer to a large stockpot and cover with the milk and stock. Bring to a simmer and cook uncovered until the asparagus is just beginning to soften, about 3 minutes. Remove from the heat, drain and transfer to a small bowl with the butter and salt. Reserve and keep warm.

For the lobster compound butter

- 1 lb (500 g) sweet butter, at room temperature
- 4 oz (100 g) lobster meat, roughly chopped
- 2 shallots, peeled and sliced thinly
- ½ bunch chervil
- 2 branches tarragon
- 1 Tbsp (15 mL) pink peppercorns
- 1 yellow pepper, roasted, skinned, seeded and chopped

In a large nonreactive bowl mix all the ingredients together with a wooden spoon, being careful not to break up the lobster meat. It should have a rustic look. On a sheet of plastic wrap about 12 inches (30 cm) long mound the butter evenly so that it runs across the width of the plastic wrap. Fold the plastic over the butter to completely cover it. Use your thumbs to evenly distribute the butter along the length of the wrap, leaving about 2 inches (5 cm) on each end. Twist at both ends in opposite directions until all the air gaps are replaced with butter. Tie each end while still keeping a tube-like shape. Refrigerate until needed.

For the lobster sauce

- 2 lb (1 kg) lobster shells
- 1 Tbsp (15 mL) corn oil
- 1 medium onion, peeled and chopped
- 1 large carrot, peeled and chopped
- 2 ribs celery, chopped
- 2 Tbsp (30 mL) tomato paste
- 1 large tomato, chopped, skin on
- 2 cloves garlic, peeled and chopped
- 4 sprigs thyme
- 2 sprigs tarragon
- ¼ cup (60 mL) brandy
- 1 cup (250 mL) white wine
- 4 cups (1 L) whipping (35%) cream
- coarse salt
- pinch of cayenne pepper

Preheat oven to 300°F (150°C).

Wash the lobster shells in cold water to remove any debris. Transfer to a sheet pan and roast on the middle rack of the oven until the shells turn a soft pink, about 30 minutes. Remove from the heat, transfer to a food processor fitted with a metal blade and pulse until the shells are coarsely chopped. Remove and reserve.

In a large saucepan over medium heat sauté the shells in the corn oil until fragrant, about 4–5 minutes. Add the onion, carrot and celery and continue to sauté until lightly caramelized, about 8 minutes. Add the tomato paste and cook until well coated. Add the chopped tomato, garlic, thyme and tarragon, and continue to cook, stirring. Carefully deglaze with the brandy and white wine, letting the alcohol ignite. After the flames have subsided add the cream and continue to cook over low heat until the sauce has reduced by half. Remove from the heat and pass through a fine mesh strainer 2–3 times. Transfer to a small saucepan and keep warm over a very low heat. Season with salt and cayenne pepper and keep warm until needed.

For the lobster fingers

- 3 oz (75 g) lobster meat, tail, claws and knuckle meat
- ¼ lb (125 g) raw tiger shrimp, peeled and deveined
- 1 tsp (5 mL) sweet butter
- 1 Tbsp (15 mL) minced yellow pepper
- 1 Tbsp (15 mL) minced poblano pepper
- 1 scallion, minced
- 1 Tbsp (15 mL) all-purpose flour
- 1 cup (250 mL) whipping (35%) cream
- 2–3 sprigs cilantro, stems removed and leaves chiffonade
- 8 lobster legs, washed and trimmed
- 2 Tbsp (30 mL) cornstarch
- 1 cup (250 mL) tempura batter
- 2–3 fresh panko breadcrumbs

Cut the lobster meat into ½-inch (1-cm) chunks. Place in a large nonreactive bowl. In a food processor fitted with a metal blade pulse the shrimp until puréed. Add to the bowl of lobster then cover and refrigerate. Melt the butter in a small sauté pan over medium heat. Add the yellow pepper, poblano pepper and scallion and sweat without adding any color, about 3 minutes. Add the flour and stir until well coated. Add the whipping cream and cook until all the liquid has evaporated, about 7–8 minutes. Remove from the heat and let cool completely. Add the cream mixture and cilantro to the bowl containing the lobster and gently mix until incorporated. Dust the meat end of the lobster leg in cornstarch and gently dip your fingers in the cornstarch. Wrap 1 oz (25 g) of lobster mixture around the leg. Use your starch-covered fingers to press the mixture firmly into an egg shape around the leg. Continue until all the fingers are completed. Fry until crisp and golden brown, about 3–4 minutes. Remove and drain on paper towels. Keep warm until ready to serve.

When ready to serve

Spoon some of the potato salad in the center of 4 warm dinner plates, place 2 trout fillets on top and garnish with white asparagus spears. Pool some of the lobster sauce to the side and garnish with a lobster finger.

shrimp

spoon bread stuffing | kick-ass tartar sauce | wilted chicory

Shrimp so big you have to eat them with a knife and fork are as satisfying as it gets.

To build the dish
shrimp
spoon bread stuffing
kick-ass tartar sauce
wilted chicory

Serves 4

For the shrimp

16 extra-large black tiger shrimp, about 2 oz (50 g) each
coarse salt
freshly ground black pepper
2 cups (500 mL) spoon bread stuffing, crumbled
2 Tbsp (30 mL) sweet butter, melted

Preheat oven to 375°F (190°C).

Place a wire rack on a sheet pan.

Peel the shrimp, keeping the tails intact and saving the remaining shells for stock. Butterfly the shrimp and remove the intestinal tract. Season with salt and pepper and place 1 Tbsp (15 mL) of spoon bread stuffing in the center of each shrimp tail. Drizzle with butter, transfer to the prepared sheet pan and broil until the stuffing is golden brown, about 3–4 minutes. Rest in a warm place until needed.

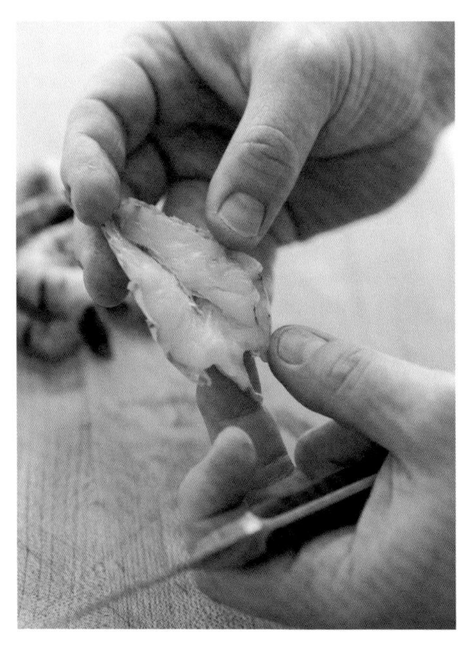

For the spoon bread stuffing

1 cup (250 mL) cooked grits
2 Tbsp (30 mL) sweet butter
¾ cup (175 mL) 2% milk
¾ cup (175 mL) white cornmeal
¾ tsp (175 mL) salt
3 eggs, separated
12 oysters, shucked and chopped
1 ear sweet corn, blanched and niblets removed
2 sprigs tarragon, stems removed
coarse salt
freshly ground black pepper

Preheat oven to 375°F (190°C).

Combine the cooked grits, butter and milk in a heavy-bottomed saucepan and slowly bring to boiling point, stirring constantly. Add the cornmeal all at once. Remove from the heat and beat well then let cool. Beat in the salt and the 3 egg yolks. Stir in the oysters, corn niblets and tarragon. Season with salt and pepper. Beat the egg whites until stiff and fold into the batter. Pour into a 9-inch (2.5-L) square non-stick pan and bake until puffed and just brown, about 20 minutes. Remove and keep warm until needed.

For the kick-ass tartar sauce

1 cup (250 mL) storebought mayonnaise
1 tsp (5 mL) smoked paprika
1 jalapeño pepper, seeded and minced
8 sprigs cilantro, stems removed and chiffonade
2 sprigs dill, stems removed
2 scallions, minced
1 Tbsp (15 mL) capers, minced
1 lemon, zest only

In a large nonreactive bowl mix all the ingredients together until incorporated. Adjust seasoning with salt and pepper. Cover and refrigerate until needed.

For the wilted chicory

4–5 cloves garlic, peeled and sliced as thinly as possible
2 shallots, peeled and sliced as thinly as possible
2 Tbsp (30 mL) olive oil
4 cups (1 L) chicory, washed and cut into 1-inch (2.5-cm) lengths
½ tsp (2 mL) crushed chilies
1 cup (250 mL) shellfish stock (recipe page 149)
coarse salt
sweet butter

In a large sauté pan over medium heat, sauté the garlic and shallots in olive oil until translucent, about 2 minutes. Add the chicory and chilies and continue to cook. Deglaze with shellfish stock and reduce until dry, about 3–4 minutes. Season with salt and butter. Keep warm until needed.

When ready to serve

Spoon some of the wilted chicory in the center of 4 warm dinner plates and top with 4 stuffed shrimp. Garnish with some kick-ass tartar sauce to the side.

pork loin

kimchi | Korean barbecue sauce | daikon noodles

I like eating this dish from little plates. You can decide how you bring the flavors together and how much heat and contrast in textures you want.

To build the dish
pork loin
kimchi
Korean barbecue sauce
daikon noodles

Serves 4

For the pork loin

28 oz (825 g) pork loin, center-cut
2 Tbsp (30 mL) sesame oil
coarse salt
1 ½ cups (375 mL) Korean barbecue sauce

Preheat oven to 350°F (180°C). Place a wire rack over a sheet pan.

Pat the pork loin dry with a kitchen towel. Drizzle with the sesame oil and rub with your hands until evenly coated. Season with salt and sear over high heat in a cast iron frying pan until caramelized on all sides. Remove from the heat and transfer to the prepared sheet pan. Generously baste with barbecue sauce and roast on the middle rack of the oven. Baste every 5 minutes until the pork loin is firm to the touch, about 25 minutes. Remove from the heat and rest in a warm place until needed.

For the kimchi

2 Chinese cabbages
1 cup (250 mL) coarse salt
5–10 spring onions, chopped very small
4 cloves garlic, peeled and crushed
2 oz (50 g) ginger, peeled and crushed
¼ cup (60 mL) Korean chili powder
2 Tbsp (30 mL) granulated sugar
1 Tbsp (15 mL) Korean kochujang paste

Rinse the cabbages, then quarter them lengthwise and discard the stems. Chop the cabbages laterally into 1-inch (2.5-cm) squares. Place the cabbage in a clean plastic bag, or equivalent, and sprinkle salt over each layer. This will create a brine solution with the cabbage juice. To ensure the cabbage is properly salted, sprinkle salt onto your wet hands then rub it into the cabbage pieces. Press the leaves in your hand to squeeze out as much water as possible. Once finished, tie up the bag and set it aside for 5–6 hours. Check after 3 hours, stirring if necessary. Take the cabbage out of the salt solution and rinse it if necessary. It should be a lot softer than before. Again, remove any surplus water. Place the cabbage in a sealable plastic container. Add the spring onions then the garlic and ginger. Add the chili powder, sugar and kochujang paste and rub into the leaves as you did with the salt. If the color doesn't seem dark enough, add more chili powder. It's a good idea to wear gloves while doing this. Refrigerate in the container for 3 days. When ready, the kimchi should be soft in consistency, but not too mushy, with a little crunchiness left in the larger pieces. Refrigerate in the covered container for up to 1 month.

For the Korean barbecue sauce

- 1 oz (25 g) ginger, peeled and minced
- 4 scallions, trimmed and minced
- 1 Tbsp (15 mL) sesame seeds, toasted
- ½ cup (125 mL) dark soy sauce
- ¼ cup (60 mL) rice wine vinegar
- 1 Tbsp (15 mL) sesame oil
- 1 cup (250 mL) ketchup
- 2 Tbsp (30 mL) Korean kochujang paste

In a small saucepan over medium heat sauté the ginger and scallions until fragrant, about 2 minutes. Add the remaining ingredients and bring to a boil. Reduce the heat and simmer until thick, about 8–10 minutes. Remove from the heat and reserve until needed.

For the daikon noodles

- 1 large daikon, washed and peeled
- 4–5 scallions, washed and julienne
- 2 oz (50 g) ginger, peeled and julienne
- 2 Tbsp (30 mL) mirin
- 1 Tbsp (15 mL) rice wine vinegar
- 1 Tbsp (15 mL) sesame oil

Use a Japanese mandoline fitted with the ¼-inch (0.5-cm) cutting blades to cut the daikon into long noodle-like strips. Place in a large nonreactive bowl and toss with the remaining ingredients. Serve immediately.

When ready to serve

On a clean work surface carve the pork loin into 4 equal portions and place on 4 warm plates. Spoon Korean barbecue sauce overtop and serve small dishes of the kimchi and daikon noodles on the side.

poussin

salt crust | Tuscan bread salad | garlic rapini

Italy meets North America in this dish of classic stuffed bird with an Italian spin. The Tuscan bread salad takes on all the flavors of this roast. If you haven't tried doing a salt crust before, this is the ideal dish to try it out!

To build the dish
poussin
salt crust
Tuscan bread salad
garlic rapini

Serves 4

For the poussin

4 poussin, about 12 oz (350 g) each
1 loaf Tuscan bread, day old preferred
2 cloves garlic, peeled and minced
1 onion, peeled and minced
1 rib celery, peeled and minced
2 Tbsp (30 mL) butter
2 sprigs sage, stems removed
4–5 sprigs flat-leaf parsley, stems removed
2 Tbsp (30 mL) pine nuts
2 Tbsp (30 mL) golden raisins
¼ tsp (1 mL) grated nutmeg
1 lemon, zest only
freshly ground black pepper
¼ cup (60 mL) olive oil
5 cups (1.25 L) salt crust

Preheat oven to 350°F (180°C).

Wash and pat dry the poussins, then refrigerate until needed. In a large bowl tear the loaf into sugar cube-sized pieces. In a large saucepan over medium heat sweat the garlic, onions and celery in the butter until translucent, about 3–4 minutes. Add the sage, parsley, pine nuts and raisins. Continue to cook for about 3 minutes then season with the nutmeg, lemon zest and pepper. Add the cubed bread and olive oil and continue to stir until completely blended. Remove from the heat and cool.

Open each bird's cavity and pack in as much stuffing as possible. Fold the wings under the birds and truss with butcher's twine. Spread 1 cup (250 mL) of salt crust on the bottom of a heavy roasting pan. Place the stuffed and trussed birds on the salt crust and pack the remaining salt crust evenly overtop the birds. Place on the middle rack of the oven and roast until the salt crust becomes golden brown and brittle, about 50 minutes. Remove and rest for 10 minutes in a warm place.

Carefully brush the salt crust off and transfer the birds to a clean work surface. Snip and discard the butcher's twine. Use a spoon to remove the stuffing and transfer to a bowl to keep warm until needed. Cut the birds in half, use kitchen scissors to remove the backbone and discard it. Keep the birds warm until needed.

For the salt crust

½ cup (125 mL) egg whites
5 cups (1.25 L) coarse salt

Use a stand or hand-held mixer to whip the egg whites to stiff peaks. Transfer to a bowl with the coarse salt and mix until evenly incorporated. Reserve at room temperature until needed.

For the Tuscan bread salad

2 cups (500 mL) finished stuffing from the poussins
1 head traverse radicchio, washed and torn into bite-size pieces
1 head arugula, washed and torn into bite-size pieces
3 Tbsp (45 mL) extra virgin olive oil
1 Tbsp (15 mL) balsamic vinegar
coarse salt
freshly ground black pepper

Toss the stuffing with the radicchio and arugula in a large bowl. Drizzle with the olive oil and balsamic vinegar. Season with salt and pepper and reserve.

For the garlic rapini

2 bunches rapini, washed, trimmed and stems peeled
¼ cup (60 mL) olive oil
8–10 cloves roasted garlic
½ tsp (2 mL) red pepper flakes
2 lemons, zest only
coarse salt
freshly ground black pepper

Chop the rapini into bite-size pieces. In a large stockpot over medium heat combine the olive oil, roasted garlic and red pepper flakes. Cook until the oil is aromatic, about 45 seconds. Be careful not to let the garlic burn. Add the rapini and stir. The volume will decrease considerably. Toss continuously to avoid browning the greens. It will take 2–3 minutes for the rapini to wilt. Season with salt and pepper. Add ½ cup (125 mL) of water and cook until it evaporates. Remove from the heat and keep warm.

When ready to serve

Mound the bread salad in the center of 4 warm dinner plates. Place 2 halves of poussin on either side of each and finish with garlic rapini.

Hot

June | July | August

When I'm Hot

June | July | August

The first time I truly understood the importance of markets was the summer I spent working in Florence. It was to be my first job as a graduate—for no pay, of course. The ink on my degree from the Culinary Institute of America was still wet as I boarded the plane. I remember the first morning at the market: it was my 26th birthday. The idea that you could pick your own live chickens in the market, take them back to the kitchen and have them prepared and ready to serve in a variety of fashions the very same day was amazing to me. Even more amazing was that this was the norm from small families to restaurants.

wild salmon

tandoori | biryani vegetables | lime pickle

You should have seen my face when I finally figured out how to portion salmon and have it cook to the same doneness all the way through! Try it once and I think you'll feel the same way.

To build the dish
salmon steaks
tandoori marinade
biryani vegetables
lime pickle
toasted poppadums

serves 4

For the salmon steaks

1 leek, cut lengthwise
1 fillet of wild salmon, center-cut, pin bones removed, about 32 oz (800 g)
8 kaffir lime leaves
2 oz ginger (50 g), peeled and sliced paper-thin
¼ cup (60 mL) cilantro leaves
¼ cup (60 mL) tandoori marinade
coarse salt

Preheat oven to 350°F (180°C)

Prepare a bowl of ice water.

In a large pot of boiling water blanch the leek until just soft, about 1 minute. Remove and submerge into the ice water. Cut into 4 equal lengths.

Cut the salmon fillet in half lengthwise along the backbone line. Place the lime leaves, ginger slices and cilantro leaves on 1 side of the salmon and sandwich together with the other side. Brush with tandoori marinade on all sides. Place 1 leek ribbon on the work surface and tie it as snugly as you can while still keeping the integrity of the steak. In a sauté pan over medium heat sear the salmon steaks until lightly caramelized, about 2 minutes. Flip and continue to cook another 1–2 minutes. Remove and transfer to a wire rack lined sheet pan. Roast until just firm, about 5–7 minutes. Remove and keep warm.

For the tandoori marinade

2 Tbsp (30 mL) tandoori paste
2 Tbsp (30 mL) olive oil
2 limes, zest only
¼ cup (60 mL) cilantro leaves

In a food processor fitted with a metal blade, blend all the ingredients together into a smooth paste. Transfer to a nonreactive container and refrigerate until needed.

For the biryani vegetables

4 Chinese long beans, blanched and shocked
2 oz (50 g) cauliflower florets, blanched and shocked
2 oz (50 g) carrot batons, blanched and shocked
2 oz (50 g) peeled butternut squash, cubed, blanched and shocked
1 oz (25 g) okra, sliced lengthwise
1 oz (25 g) ginger, peeled and julienne
1 scallion, julienne
1 oz (25 g) clarified butter
1 oz (25 g) biryani paste
coarse salt

In a large nonreactive bowl mix together the long beans, cauliflower, carrots, squash, okra, ginger and scallion. Keep on hand. In a large sauté pan over low heat add the clarified butter and biryani paste. Mix with a wooden spoon until a fragrant and smooth paste develops. Add the mixed vegetables and increase the heat to medium. Gently toss the vegetables until evenly coated in the spice paste. Continue to sauté until the slightest color starts to appear on the vegetables. Remove from the heat and season with salt. Keep warm until needed.

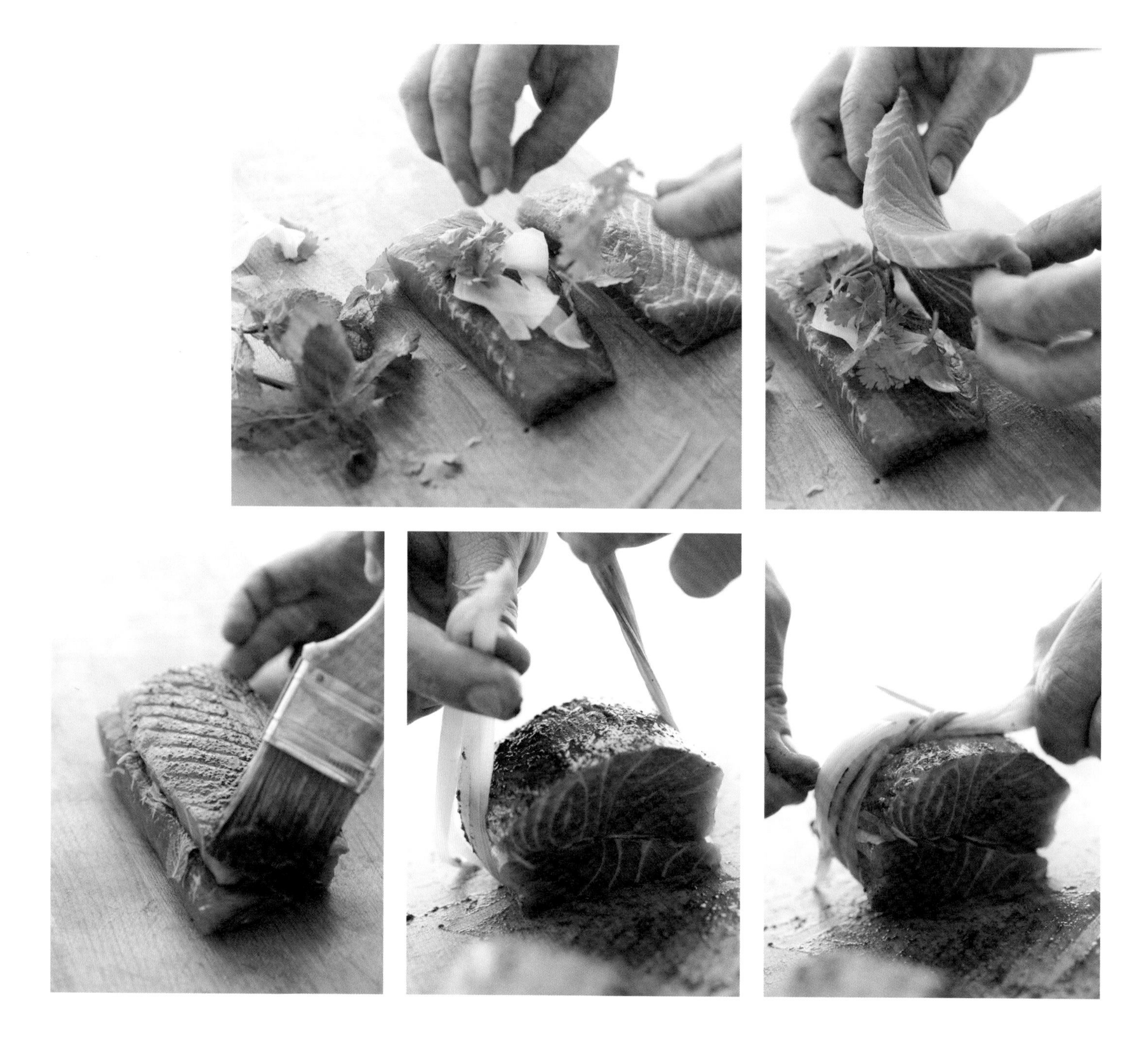

wild salmon (continued)

For the lime pickle

4 limes, washed and diced
¼ cup (60 mL) vegetable oil
1 tsp (5 mL) yellow mustard seeds
½ tsp (2 mL) fenugreek seeds
½ cup (125 mL) dried curry leaves, loosely packed
½ cup (125 mL) fresh lime juice
1 tsp (5 mL) ground turmeric
1 tsp (5 mL) cayenne pepper
1 tsp (5 mL) salt

In a small saucepan over high heat blanch the diced limes in boiling water for 1 minute. Discard the cooking liquid and repeat 2–3 more times. Put the limes in fresh water and boil again, this time for 30 minutes. The limes should become tender and lose their bright green color. Drain and set aside.

In a large saucepan over low heat add the vegetable oil, mustard seeds and fenugreek seeds. Sauté until the seeds just start to pop. Quickly add the curry leaves, lime juice, turmeric, cayenne pepper and salt. Add the cooked limes and remove from the heat. Stir to incorporate everything. In a food processor fitted with a metal blade, purée until smooth. Remove from the food processor, let cool completely and store in a clean glass container.

For the toasted poppadums

8 black pepper poppadums

Preheat broiler to 500°F (260°C).

Warm 1 poppadum on the back of a small sheet pan under broiler for 5 seconds. Remove from the heat and place on a clean cutting board. With the tip of a sharp French knife cut the poppadum in half. Return to the broiler and toast until the poppadum starts to bubble and little dark spots appear. Remove from the broiler and wrap around a rolling pin to shape. Let cool completely and store uncovered until needed.

When ready to serve

Use a pallet knife to spread equal portions of lime pickle over 4 warm dinner plates. Place a salmon steak at one end of the pickle and the biryani vegetables at the other end. Garnish each plate with 2 toasted poppadums.

red snapper

coconut-curry tea | ginger hay | super-jumbo shrimp roll

Every so often you have to eat a fish with its head on. It should remind us that people do everything in their power to get that fish from hook to plate as fast as possible.

To build the dish
red snapper
coconut-curry tea
ginger hay
super-jumbo shrimp roll
sesame dressing
sesame pea tendrils

Serves 4

For the red snapper

4 red snappers, washed and scaled, about 14–16 oz (400–450 g) each
2 limes, washed and sliced as thinly as possible
6 cloves garlic, peeled and sliced thinly
2 oz (50 g) ginger, peeled and sliced paper-thin
2 Thai bird chilies, split
2 Tbsp (30 mL) grape seed oil
1 tsp (5 mL) coarse salt

Preheat broiler to 500°F (260°C). Place a wire rack over a sheet pan.

Slash the flesh of the snapper parallel to the gills from head to tail. Flip and repeat on the other side. Sporadically stuff each slit with lime, garlic and ginger slices. Take one of the bird chilies and rub it all over the snapper. Drizzle the snapper with the oil and season with salt. Transfer to the prepared sheet pan and broil on the bottom rack of the oven until the fish is firm to the touch, about 10 minutes. If the fish gets too dark cover it with aluminum foil. Remove from the oven and rest in a warm place.

For the coconut-curry tea

½ cup (125 mL) fresh coconut meat
1 Tbsp (15 mL) yellow curry paste
1 tsp (5 mL) freshly grated turmeric
4–5 kaffir lime leaves
1 stalk lemon grass
4 cups (1 L) white fish stock, boiling (recipe page 150)

In a mortar and pestle blend the coconut, yellow curry paste and turmeric until smooth.

Remove and transfer to a heatproof teapot. Add the lime leaves and lemon grass. Fill with the boiling stock and steep for 5 minutes. Reserve and keep warm until needed.

For the ginger hay

½ lb (250 g) fresh ginger, peeled and julienne
vegetable oil for frying
coarse salt

Preheat deep-fryer to 375°F (190°C).

Sprinkle the julienne ginger into the deep-fryer and gently swish from side to side. Fry until golden brown, about 3 minutes. Remove when the bubbles have almost stopped and transfer to a paper towel-lined bowl. Season with coarse salt and keep warm until needed.

For the super-jumbo shrimp roll

- 1 lb (500 g) black tiger shrimp, about 24
- 4 extra-large rice paper wrappers
- 1 cup (250 mL) vegetable shred (recipe page 151)
- 2 oz (50 g) barbecue pork, julienne
- ½ cup (125 mL) Thai basil leaves
- ½ cup (125 mL) mint leaves
- ½ cup (125 mL) cilantro leaves
- 2 oz (60 mL) sesame dressing

In a bamboo steamer over boiling water steam the shrimp until firm to the touch, about 1 minute. Remove from the heat and cool completely. Fill a shallow baking dish, large enough to accommodate the rice paper wrappers, with very hot tap water and soak the wrappers until soft. Use a kitchen towel to pat the excess moisture from the rice paper. Place 6 poached shrimp in the center of each wrapper. Place ¼ cup (60 mL) of the vegetable shred on top of the shrimp. Place 1/2 oz (6 g) of the barbecue pork on this. Finish with the Thai basil, mint leaves and cilantro. Drizzle with a little of the sesame dressing. Fold both sides over so they overlap. The rice paper wrapper should now be 3 inches (7.5 cm) wide. Bring the bottom up and gently roll with a little bit of tension. Rice paper wrappers have a natural stickiness to them but you will have to let them rest, seam sides down, on a damp kitchen towel in the refrigerator for about 20 minutes. And then they are ready to serve.

For the sesame dressing

- 5 Tbsp (75 mL) white sesame seeds
- 1 tsp (5 mL) mirin
- 1 tsp (5 mL) soy sauce
- 2 Tbsp (30 mL) dashi

Place the sesame seeds in a dry heavy saucepan or frying pan and parch them over low heat, shaking the pan constantly, until their aroma is released and a few seeds begin to jump out of the pan. Remove from the heat. Dampen a non-terry kitchen towel and lightly wring it out. Place a clean, dry suribachi on the towel, add the hot, parched sesame seeds and grind them. As you grind, sesame oil will be released and the seeds will form a sticky paste. Scrape the grooves of the suribachi with a bamboo skewer and gather the paste in the center. Add the mirin, soy sauce and dashi and mix well. Use the dressing as it is or, if you prefer a smoother consistency, force the mixture through a fine mesh sieve.

For the sesame pea tendrils

- 2 cups (500 mL) snow pea tendrils
- 2 Tbsp (30 mL) sesame dressing
- 1 tsp (5 mL) sesame seeds

In a large nonreactive bowl, mix all ingredients together gently with your hands so as not to bruise the snow peas. Set aside.

When ready to serve

Divide the coconut-curry tea equally into 4 warm dinner bowls and place a snapper on each. Garnish with sesame pea tendrils and ginger hay. Serve the super-jumbo shrimp rolls on the side.

pickerel

cedar jelly | fiddleheads | rosemary smokies

Pickerel is the king of the north when it comes to freshwater fish. I have yet to taste a sweeter fish.

To build the dish
pickerel
cedar jelly
fiddleheads
rosemary smokies

Serves 4

For the pickerel

2 lb (1 kg) pickerel fillets, pin bones removed
1 Tbsp (15 mL) vegetable oil
coarse salt
freshly ground white pepper

Drizzle the pickerel fillets with the vegetable oil and season with salt and pepper. Reserve.

For the cedar jelly

½ cup (125 mL) cedar jelly
¼ cup (60 mL) sweet butter, at room temperature
4 untreated cedar planks

Preheat oven to 475°F (240°C).

In a small nonreactive bowl combine the cedar jelly and sweet butter until smooth. Using a pastry brush, spread the mixture in the center of the cedar planks, about the size of the pickerel fillets. Place a pickerel on the buttered surface of each plank. Transfer to the middle rack of the oven. Roast until firm to the touch, about 5 minutes depending on the thickness of the fish. Remove the plank from the oven and tent with aluminum foil.

For the fiddleheads

1 lb (500 g) fiddlehead ferns
2 Tbsp (30 mL) sweet butter
2 cloves garlic, peeled and smashed
coarse salt to taste

Prepare a bowl of ice water.

In a large stockpot full of boiling salted water, cook the fiddleheads until bright green. Remove from the water with a wire strainer and shock in the ice water. Remove from the ice water and drain. Reserve.

In a medium sauté pan over low heat, melt the butter and add the smashed garlic. Add the fiddleheads and gently warm them through. Adjust seasoning with coarse salt. Remove from the heat and reserve in a warm place.

For the rosemary smokies

1½ lb (750 g) fingerling potatoes
2 lemons, washed and sliced thinly
1 bunch rosemary
1 head of garlic, split
2 Tbsp (30 mL) olive oil
coarse salt
freshly ground black pepper

Preheat oven to 350°F (180°C).

Wash and scrub the potatoes. Transfer to a cutting board and slice the potatoes in half lengthwise. Reserve.

Lay 2 feet (60 cm) of aluminum foil across a clean work surface. Lay sliced lemons in a 3- x 12-inch (7.5- x 30-cm) pattern and top with rosemary branches and smashed garlic. Place the fingerling potatoes on top of this in an orderly fashion. Drizzle with olive oil and season with salt and pepper. Bring the top and bottom of the foil together and fold over a couple of times. Fold the ends so you have a tight long package. Transfer to the middle rack of the oven and bake until the potatoes are soft to the touch about 30 minutes, depending on the size. Remove from the oven and reserve in a warm place.

When ready to serve

Divide the fiddleheads and rosemary smokies equally in the center of 4 warm dinner plates. Place pickerel fillets on each and garnish with cedar jelly.

yellow fin tuna

cool | warm | hot

This is the dish that changed the way I thought about how to put food on a plate. The trio has almost replaced tasting menus as a way to showcase food.

To build the dish
tuna cool
tuna warm
gazpacho sauce
tuna hot

Serves 4

For the tuna cool

½ lb (225 g) tuna trim, cut into small dice
12 extra-large green olives, halved and pits removed
1 lemon, zest only
4 fillets white anchovies, chopped
5–6 basil leaves, chiffonade
2 Tbsp (30 mL) extra virgin olive oil
1 Tbsp (15 mL) sherry vinegar
4–5 cloves roasted garlic, smashed
coarse salt
freshly ground white pepper

In a large nonreactive bowl mix all the ingredients together and let stand at room temperature to marry all the flavors. Cover and reserve.

For the tuna warm

1 lb (500 g) center-cut tuna
1 Tbsp (15 mL) olive oil
1 green zucchini, sliced as thinly as possible into ribbons
1 yellow zucchini, sliced as thinly as possible into ribbons
2 Tbsp (30 mL) sun-dried tomato spread (recipe page 151)
8 large basil leaves
1 cup (250 mL) gazpacho sauce

Cut the tuna into logs, about 1 x 1 x 3 inches (2.5 x 2.5 x 7.5 cm). Rub the tuna with the olive oil and set aside. In a cast iron frying pan over high heat sear the tuna log on all sides until lightly charred, about 15 seconds per side. Remove and reserve.

In the same pan, or a grill pan if you have one, lightly char the zucchini ribbons on both sides and quickly remove them from the pan and let cool. Lay the zucchini ribbons in alternating colors to form a 3- x 6-inch (7.5- x 15-cm) rectangle. Spread 1½ tsp (7 mL) of sun-dried tomato purée on each zucchini mat and top with a basil leaf or 2, depending on their size. Place a tuna log on each mat and roll with a little bit of tension. Cover and reserve.

For the gazpacho sauce

2 red Roma tomatoes
2 yellow tomatoes
1 yellow pepper, roasted, peeled and chopped
1 small cucumber, peeled, seeded and chopped
3 scallions, white only, minced
1 tsp (5 mL) piri-piri-style hot sauce
2 Tbsp (30 mL) extra virgin olive oil
coarse salt
1 lemon, juice and zest

Prepare a bowl of ice water.

Score the bottom of the tomatoes with a paring knife and blanch in boiling water until you can see the skin separating from the flesh, about 15 seconds. Quickly remove with a wire strainer and plunge into the ice water to stop the cooking process. Carefully peel and discard the skins. Cut the tomato in half and gently squeeze the seeds and juice over a fine mesh strainer to separate. Discard the seeds and reserve the tomato water. Dice and place in a large nonreactive bowl. Add the remaining ingredients and stir until well mixed. Cover and keep at room temperature until needed.

yellow fin tuna (continued)

For the tuna hot

- 2 canned piquillo peppers
- 1 tsp (5 mL) smoked paprika
- 2 cups (500 mL) vegetable stock (recipe page 150)
- 1 shallot, peeled and sliced
- 1 clove garlic, peeled and smashed
- 1 Tbsp (15 mL) olive oil
- 1 cup (250 mL) short-grain rice
- 1 dry cured chorizo sausage
- 16 small pasta clams, scrubbed
- 4 oz (100 g) tuna, sliced as thinly as possible
- 8 black tiger shrimp, 21–25 count, peeled and deveined

In a food processor fitted with a metal blade, pulse the piquillo peppers, smoked paprika and vegetable stock until smooth, about 60 seconds. Remove and reserve. In a saucepan over medium heat sauté the shallot and garlic in the olive oil until translucent, about 2 minutes. Add the rice and stir until coated. Add the piquillo pepper purée and bring to a boil. Reduce the heat to low and cover. Cook, covered, for 15 minutes and then add the clams and sausage. Continue cooking for 3–4 minutes and then add the shrimp. Continue to cook until the clams have opened and the shrimp have turned pink. Remove from the heat and fold in the sliced tuna. Cover and keep warm until needed.

When ready to serve

Spoon equal amounts of the gazpacho sauce in the center of 4 warm dinner plates. On a clean work surface slice the tuna logs into 3 pieces and place on top of the sauce. To one side of this spoon some of the tuna cool olive salad and on the opposite side some of the tuna hot rice.

beef tenderloin

asparagus | buttermilk onion rings | lobster butter

People will think you're cooking them beef tenderloin because you think they're special but really, it's just an excuse to make the onion rings. Don't tell!

To build the dish
beef tenderloin
smoky rub
red wine jus
asparagus
classic hollandaise
lobster butter
buttermilk onion rings

Serves 4

For the beef tenderloin

four ½-lb (250-g) beef tenderloin fillets
1 Tbsp (15 mL) smoky rub
1 Tbsp (15 mL) olive oil
coarse salt

Preheat grill to high.

Place the fillets on a clean work surface and sprinkle with smoky rub. Drizzle with the olive oil and use your hands to rub it in until the beef is well coated. Season with salt and transfer to the hot grill. Cook for 5–6 minutes per side for medium-rare. Remove from the heat and rest in a warm place.

For the smoky rub

2 Tbsp (30 mL) smoked paprika
1 tsp (5 mL) chili powder
1 tsp (5 mL) freshly ground black pepper
½ tsp (2 mL) dried mustard
½ tsp (2 mL) brown sugar
½ tsp (2 mL) cayenne pepper

Mix together all the ingredients and store in a covered container in a cool, dry place.

For the red wine jus

1 Tbsp (15 mL) vegetable oil
¼ cup (60 mL) onion, medium dice
2 Tbsp (30 mL) carrot, medium dice
1 rib celery, medium dice
2 Tbsp (30 mL) tomato paste
4 cups (1 L) veal jus (recipe page 150)
1 bottle (750 mL) red wine

Heat the oil in a large saucepan over medium-high heat, add the onion, carrot and celery and sauté until golden brown, about 10 minutes. Add the tomato paste and continue to cook until the vegetables are well coated, about 3 minutes. Deglaze with the veal jus and red wine. Reduce the heat to low and simmer until reduced to ¼ of its original volume. Remove from the heat, strain through a fine mesh sieve and then pass through cheesecloth. Reserve uncovered and keep warm until needed.

For the asparagus

1 lb (500 g) very thin asparagus
1 Tbsp (15 mL) sweet butter
coarse salt
1 cup (250 mL) classic hollandaise

Prepare a bowl of ice water.

Holding the asparagus by the tip, gently peel the spears, being careful to keep their shape. Tie all the spears in a loose bundle with butcher's twine then blanch until bright green, about 1 minute, in a large pot of salted boiling water. Remove from the pot and stop the cooking process by submerging in the ice water. Remove and drain. When ready to serve, warm the spears in a small sauté pan over low heat with the butter. Season with salt and serve with the warm hollandaise.

beef tenderloin (continued)

For the classic hollandaise

- 2 Tbsp (30 mL) white wine vinegar
- ¼ cup (60 mL) boiling water
- 3 large egg yolks
- ½ cup (125 mL) clarified butter, melted
- ¼ tsp (1 mL) Tabasco sauce
- ½ tsp (2 mL) salt

In a small saucepan over low heat warm the white wine vinegar. Remove from the heat and reserve. Prepare another saucepan with boiling water and a measuring tablespoon. Place the top of a double boiler over but not in the hot water. Place the egg yolks in the top of the double boiler and whisk until they begin to thicken. Now add 1 Tbsp (15 mL) of the boiling water. Continue to whisk the sauce until it begins to thicken. Repeat with the remaining water, 1 Tbsp (15 mL) at a time, beating the mixture after each addition.

Now add the warm vinegar. Remove the double boiler from the heat. Beat the sauce briskly with a wire whisk. Continue to beat the mixture as you slowly pour in the melted butter. Add the Tabasco and salt and beat the sauce until thick. Keep warm until ready to serve.

For the lobster butter

- 1 lb (500 g) sweet butter, at room temperature
- 4 oz (100 g) lobster meat, roughly chopped
- 2 shallots, peeled and sliced thinly
- ½ bunch chervil
- 2 branches tarragon
- 1 Tbsp (15 mL) pink peppercorns
- 1 yellow pepper, roasted, skinned, seeded and chopped

In a large nonreactive bowl mix all the ingredients together with a wooden spoon, being careful not to break up the lobster meat. This should have a rustic look. On a sheet of plastic wrap about 12 inches (30 cm) long, mound the butter evenly so that it runs across the width of the plastic wrap. Fold the plastic over the butter to completely cover it. Use your thumbs to evenly distribute the butter along the length of the wrap, leaving about 2 inches (5 cm) on each end. Twist at both ends in opposite directions until any air gaps are replaced with butter. Tie each end while still keeping a tube-like shape. Refrigerate for up to 1 month, slice ¼ inch (0.5 cm) thick for using.

For the buttermilk onion rings

- 6 cups (1.5 L) all-purpose flour
- 2 cups (500 mL) cornstarch
- 2 Tbsp (30 mL) smoky rub
- 2 Tbsp (30 mL) coarse salt
- 4 cups (1 L) buttermilk
- 4 medium white onions, peeled
- vegetable oil for deep-frying

In a large stainless steel bowl combine 3 cups (750 mL) of the flour, 1 cup (250 mL) of the cornstarch, 1 Tbsp (15 mL) of the smoky rub and 1 Tbsp (15 mL) of the coarse salt. Whisk until evenly incorporated. Reserve, covered, until needed.

Preheat deep-fryer to 350°F (180°C).

In a nonreactive bowl add the remaining flour, cornstarch, smoky rub and salt. Add the buttermilk and whisk into a smooth batter. Cut the onions into rings about ½-inch (1-cm) thick. With your fingers, take the onion slices and pop them into rings. For best results use the larger outer rings. Place the rings in the batter and gently toss until completely coated. With your thumb and index finger pick up the battered rings one at a time and gently flip in the dredge until completely covered in a dry coating. Place on a clean work surface and repeat until all the rings have been coated. Deep-fry until golden brown, about 4–5 minutes. Remove from the oil and drain on paper towel. Season with salt and serve immediately.

When ready to serve

Place the beef tenderloin in the center of 4 warm dinner plates and spoon some of the red wine jus overtop. Place a slice of lobster butter on the steak. Finish with asparagus spears and hollandaise and garnish with buttermilk onion rings.

ancho rabbit

pozole-poblano stew | epazote-hominy ensalada

People get a bit creeped out when you serve rabbit in its natural state. That's why this dish is so great. People don't know they're eating rabbit until they're almost finished.

To build the dish
pozole-poblano stew
epazote-hominy ensalada
ancho paint
rabbit loins
corn husk baskets

Serves 4

For the pozole-poblano stew

4 rabbit legs, front and hind
coarse salt
1 Tbsp (15 mL) corn oil
1 medium onion, peeled and minced
4 cloves garlic, peeled and minced
1 smoked jalapeño pepper (chipotle)
1 Tbsp (15 mL) epazote, chopped
4 cups (1 L) dark chicken stock (recipe page 148)
4 ancho chilies
2 poblano peppers, roasted, skinned and diced
1 cup (250 mL) cooked pozole
½ cup (125 mL) cilantro leaves

Preheat oven to 300°F (150°C).

Season the rabbit legs with salt. Heat the corn oil in a large ovenproof saucepan over medium-high heat and sear the legs until golden brown on all sides, about 3 minutes. Stir in the onion and sauté until transparent, about 3 minutes. Add the garlic, chipotle and epazote and continue to cook, stirring. Add 3 cups (750 mL) of the chicken stock and bring to a boil. Cover and transfer to the middle rack of the oven and braise for 40 minutes.

Remove and discard the stems from the ancho chilies. Combine with the remaining chicken stock in a small saucepan and bring to a boil over high heat. Reduce the heat and simmer until the ancho chilies are very soft, about 15 minutes. Transfer to a food processor fitted with a metal blade and purée until smooth. Remove the rabbit from the oven and add the ancho purée, poblano peppers and pozole. Cover, return to the oven and continue to braise for 20 minutes.

Remove from the oven and let cool for 20 minutes. Carefully remove the rabbit legs and place on a clean work surface. Separate the meat from the bone. Reserve the meat and discard the bones. Bring the braising liquid back to a boil over high heat and reduce by half. Reduce the heat to low, add the reserved leg meat and continue to simmer for 3–5 minutes. Remove from the heat and adjust the seasoning with salt. Add the cilantro leaves just before serving.

For the epazote-hominy ensalada

1 cup (250 mL) cooked hominy
2 Tbsp (30 mL) epazote, chopped
1 small yellow pepper, roasted, skinned and diced
2 scallions, minced
1 lime, juice and zest
2 Tbsp (30 mL) extra virgin olive oil
coarse salt
freshly ground black pepper

In a large nonreactive bowl mix together the hominy, epazote, diced pepper and scallions. Add the lime juice, zest and olive oil and toss until everything is well coated. Season to taste with salt and pepper. Refrigerate, covered, until needed.

ancho rabbit (continued)

For the ancho paint

- 4–5 dried ancho chilies
- 6 cups (1.5 L) boiling water
- 1 Tbsp (15 mL) honey
- 1 tsp (5 mL) grated Mexican chocolate

In a large stainless steel bowl cover the ancho chilies in boiling water. Let them soften, about 30 minutes. Remove the anchos and reserve about ¼ cup (60 mL) of the liquid. Use your hands to remove the stems and seeds and discard. Repeat until all the anchos are cleaned.

In a food processor fitted with a metal blade, blend the cleaned anchos with the reserved cooking liquid to form a smooth paste. Remove and pass through a fine mesh sieve over a large bowl, discarding any skin and seeds. Use a wooden spoon to blend in the honey and grated chocolate. Refrigerate, covered, until needed.

For the rabbit loins

- 2–3 slices Serrano ham
- 2 boneless rabbit loins
- 1 Tbsp (15 mL) olive oil
- 2–3 sprigs cilantro
- coarse salt
- freshly ground black pepper

Place a piece of plastic wrap about 12 inches (30 cm) square on a clean work surface. Carefully overlap the ham to form a 3- x 5-inch (7.5- x 12.5-cm) rectangle. Place the rabbit loins in the center and drizzle with olive oil. Season with cilantro leaves, salt and pepper. Roll the rabbit into a log shape. Twist both ends tightly to help hold the shape. Refrigerate for 30 minutes.

Preheat oven to 400°F (200°C). Line a sheet pan witih silicone.

Carefully unwrap the rabbit loins, being sure to keep their shape. Transfer to the prepared sheet pan. Bake on the middle rack of oven until firm to the touch, about 7 minutes. Remove and rest in a warm place. Slice into medallions for plating.

For the corn husk baskets

- 13 dried corn husks
- 12 lemons

In a large stainless steel bowl, pour boiling water over the corn husks and soak for 30 minutes. Take 1 corn husk and tear it into long, thin strips. You will need a lot of these. Keep them submerged. Place a corn husk over a lemon, pinch one end and tie with a few cornhusk strands. Repeat on the other end. Trim both ends neatly with scissors. Dry the corn husks on the lemons, this will give you the desired basket shape. Remove the lemons once the corn husks are completely dry.

When ready to serve

Use a pastry brush to apply a streak of ancho paint down the center of 4 warm dinner plates. Fill one corn husk basket with pozole-poblano stew and another with the ensalada and place on the ancho paint. On a clean work surface slice the rabbit loins in half and place on the paint. Repeat for each plate.

pork chop

baby bok choy | black bean clams | kumquat-garlic sauce

Pork is mild enough to support some pretty bold flavors. I love the combination of salty clams and fermented black beans.

To build the dish
double-cut pork chops
stir-fry paste
baby bok choy
black bean clams
kumquat-garlic sauce
crispy noodles

Serves 4

For the double-cut pork chops

2 double-cut pork chops, frenched, each about 1 lb (450 g)
1 Tbsp (15 mL) stir-fry paste
1 Tbsp (15 mL) sesame oil
coarse salt

Preheat oven to 350°F (180°C). Place a wire rack over a sheet pan.

Tie the double-cut pork chops with butcher's twine between the bones to help keep their shape. Rub the stir-fry paste over the pork chops until it is evenly distributed. Heat the sesame oil in a sauté pan over medium heat and cook the chops for 3 minutes on each side. Be careful not to burn the paste, you want only a light char. Remove from the heat, transfer to the prepared sheet pan and place on the middle rack in the oven. Roast for 10–12 minutes. Remove from the oven and rest in a warm place until needed.

For the stir-fry paste

1 oz (25 g) ginger, peeled and minced
6 cloves garlic, peeled and minced
2 Thai bird chilies, split and seeds removed
1 cup (250 mL) loosely packed cilantro leaves
1 tsp (5 mL) sesame oil
¼ cup (60 mL) canola oil

In a food processor fitted with a metal blade, pulse together all the ingredients to form a smooth paste. Remove and store in an airtight plastic container in the refrigerator until needed.

For the baby bok choy

6–8 heads baby bok choy
1 tsp (5 mL) sesame oil
1 Tbsp (15 mL) stir-fry paste
2 Tbsp (30 mL) Chinese cooking wine

On a Japanese mandoline set to ⅛-inch (3-mm) thickness, slice each baby bok choy bulb until all the bok choy is sliced. Place all the sliced bok choy in a large bowl. Add the sesame oil and stir-fry paste. Mix until well coated.

In a large sauté pan over high heat quickly sear the bok choy mixture until aromatic, about 30 seconds. Carefully deglaze with the cooking wine. Toss until the wine has evaporated, about 15 seconds. Remove from the heat and keep warm until needed.

pork chop (continued)

For the black bean clams

- 1 lb (500 g) pasta clams
- 1 tsp (5 mL) cornmeal
- 1 tsp (5 mL) sesame oil
- 1 Tbsp (15 mL) stir-fry paste
- 2 pieces star anise
- 1 Tbsp (15 mL) fermented black beans
- ½ cup (125 mL) plum wine
- ½ cup (125 mL) veal jus (recipe page 150)

Place the clams and cornmeal in a large bowl, run under water and let the clams take in some of the cornmeal. This helps the clams to purge any sand they might have inside. Wash any remaining cornmeal off the clams. Reserve until needed.

In a large sauté pan over medium-high heat, bring the sesame oil almost to its smoke point. Carefully add the clams then the stir-fry paste. Quickly toss to evenly coat the clams. Be careful not to burn the paste. Add the star anise, black beans and plum wine. Cover and steam the clams until just opened, about 2 minutes. Add the veal jus and adjust the seasoning if needed.

For the kumquat-garlic sauce

- ½ cup (125 mL) granulated sugar
- ½ cup (125 mL) kumquats, washed and cut in half (about 12–15 pieces)
- ½ cup (125 mL) garlic cloves, peeled
- 1 lime, juice only
- 2 Tbsp (30 mL) orange brandy

In a small saucepan over medium heat the sugar with 2 Tbsp (30 mL) of water. Cook, stirring often, until the sugar has melted and turns light brown. Quickly and carefully add the kumquats and garlic, stirring to coat them with the caramel. Add 6 Tbsp (90 mL) of water and continue to cook, stirring, until all the sugar is dissolved, about 3 minutes. Add the lime juice and cook until the mixture has come to a boil. Reduce the heat, add the brandy and continue to simmer, stirring, until all the liquid has evaporated, about 6 minutes. Remove from the heat, let cool completely and store in an airtight plastic container in the refrigerator until needed.

For the crispy noodles

- vegetable oil for frying
- 24 strands dried angel hair pasta

Preheat deep-fryer to 375°F (190°C). Line a bowl with paper towel.

When the fryer is ready, carefully sprinkle the dried pasta into the hot oil. Fry until crispy and most of the bubbling has stopped, about 30 seconds. Remove and transfer to the prepared bowl. Reserve, uncovered, until needed.

When ready to serve

Place a small mound of the stir-fried baby bok choy in the center of each of 4 warm dinner plates. On a clean work surface slice the double pork chops in half and place on top. Pour some of the black bean clams over and garnish with kumquat-garlic sauce and crispy noodles.

crispy flat chicken

fajita vegetables | mole rub | tortilla fries

The only real work involved in this dish is deboning the chicken. The rest is easy because the vegetables are cooked by the chicken.

To build the dish
crispy flat chicken
fajita vegetables
mole rub
tortilla fries

Serves 4

For the crispy flat chicken

2 whole chickens, about 2 ½ lb (1 kg) each
4–5 cloves garlic, peeled and sliced as thinly as possible
¼ cup (60 mL) cilantro leaves
1 jalapeño pepper, sliced as thinly as possible
coarse salt
¼ cup (60 mL) mole rub

Place the chickens breast side up on a clean, flat work surface. Use your index finger to find the sternum. Run a boning knife along the sternum and remove the breast from the rib cage. Now remove the leg from the carcass at the hip joint. With the leg flat, run your knife along both sides of the bone, being careful not to cut all the way through. Remove the leg meat from the bone and run your fingers over the surface of the meat to see if any cartilage was left behind. Remove if so. Between 2 sheets of plastic wrap, carefully pound both the breast and the boneless leg with the flat side of a meat mallet until the flesh is even and about ½ inch (1 cm) thick. Repeat until all the portions have been flattened. Use your index finger to carefully separate the flesh from the skin and make little pockets. Stuff the pockets with a couple of garlic slices, cilantro leaves and jalapeño slices. Repeat until you have evenly distributed the flavorings under the skin. With the meat side up, season with salt and brush on the mole rub. Reserve, covered, in the refrigerator.

For the fajita vegetables

1 red pepper, washed and sliced into ¼-inch (0.5-cm) rings
1 yellow pepper, washed and cut into ¼-inch (0.5-cm) rings
1 poblano pepper, washed and cut into ¼-inch (0.5-cm) rings
4 scallions, washed and trimmed into 3-inch (7.5-cm) batons

Preheat oven to 450°F (230°C).

In a large bowl, toss all the vegetables together. On an unlined sheet pan, arrange the vegetables in 4 piles. Place a flattened chicken on each pile and transfer to the middle rack of the oven. Bake until the skin is crispy and firm to the touch, about 10 minutes.

For the mole rub

1 cup (250 mL) prepared dried mole
2 limes, juice only
½ bunch cilantro, picked and washed
¼ cup (60 mL) corn oil

In a food processor fitted with a metal blade, blend all the ingredients into a smooth paste, about 1 minute. Remove and refrigerate, covered, until needed.

crispy flat chicken (continued)

For the tortilla fries

- ½ lb (250 g) fresh corn tortillas
- corn oil for deep-frying
- coarse salt

Preheat deep-fryer to 375°F (190°C). Line a bowl with paper towel.

Stack the tortillas about 4 or 5 high. With a heavy blade French knife, slice as thinly as possible. Use your hands to carefully break them apart into individual strands. Sprinkle the strands into the fryer and gently toss from side to side with a wire strainer to help cook quickly and evenly. Remove and transfer to the prepared bowl. Season with salt and reserve in a warm place.

When ready to serve

Spread some of the mole rub in the center of each of 4 warm dinner plates with a pallet knife. Place fajita vegetables and a half chicken on top of the rub and garnish with tortilla fries.

quails

creamed corn | frisée salad | Creole yams

I didn't eat a lot of quails when I was growing up, but I sure got my fill of quail-hunting stories from Peter, my Texan roommate in college at the Culinary Institute of America, New York. As you can see, there's a mess of Texas in this dish.

To build the dish
quails
coffee barbecue sauce
creamed corn
frisée salad
bacon fat vinaigrette
Creole yams

Serves 4

For the quails

8 jumbo quails, washed and patted dry
1 tsp (5 mL) corn oil
½ cup (125 mL) coffee barbecue sauce
coarse salt
freshly ground black pepper

Preheat oven to 475°F (240°C). Place a wire rack over a sheet pan.

Place each quail on its side. With a boning knife, find the backbone and remove. Press flat to remove the sternum and rib cage.

Drizzle the quails lightly with corn oil and rub in. Transfer to the prepared sheet pan and place in the middle of the oven. Bake at high heat until the skin begins to bubble, about 2–3 minutes. Flip the quails and start basting with the barbecue sauce. Continue basting, being careful not to burn the sauce. Remove when the breast is firm to the touch, about 4–5 minutes, depending on the thickness of the quails. Remove and keep covered in a warm place.

For the coffee barbecue sauce

1 Tbsp (5 mL) corn oil
½ cup (125 mL) minced onions
1 cup (250 mL) ketchup
¼ cup (60 mL) Worcestershire sauce
1 Tbsp (15 mL) sherry vinegar
½ cup (125 mL) strong coffee
2 Tbsp (30 mL) molasses
1 Tbsp (15 mL) grainy mustard
1 jalapeño pepper, seeded and minced
coarse salt
1 tsp (5 mL) liquid smoke

Preheat oven to 350°F (180°C).

In a large ovenproof saucepan heat the oil over medium heat and sweat the onion until soft and translucent. Combine the remaining ingredients and bring to a boil. Remove from the heat, cover and transfer to the middle rack of the oven. Bake for 30 minutes. Remove from the heat and let cool. Pass through a fine mesh strainer and refrigerate, covered, until needed.

For the creamed corn

4 ears sweet corn
1 bay leaf
1 tsp (5 mL) corn oil
1 yellow pepper, roasted, seeded and chopped
2 scallions, white only, minced
½ cup (125 mL) lima beans
1 cup (250 mL) whipping (35%) cream
coarse salt
freshly ground white pepper

In a large stockpot full of boiling water, blanch the corn until bright yellow, about 2 minutes. Remove from the boiling water with a wire strainer and let cool on the countertop. When cool to the touch, carefully remove the niblets with a French knife and reserve them in a bowl. Break the cobs in half with your hands and place in a small stockpot with a bay leaf. Cover with water and bring to a simmer. Cook for 30 minutes, remove from the heat and let cool completely.

In a small sauté pan over medium heat, sauté the corn niblets in oil then add the yellow pepper, scallions and lima beans. Continue to cook for 3–5 minutes. Add 1 cup (250 mL) of corn stock and cook until all the liquid has almost evaporated, about 4–5 minutes. Add the whipping cream and reduce the heat to low. Gently cook until the mixture has thickened, about another 5 minutes. Adjust the seasoning with salt and pepper and remove from the heat. Keep covered in a warm place until needed.

For the frisée salad

3 cups (750 mL) blond frisée lettuce, washed and spun dry
1 cup (250 mL) vegetable shred (recipe page 151)
¼ cup (60 mL) bacon fat vinaigrette
coarse salt
freshly ground black pepper

Place the frisée and vegetable shred in a large nonreactive bowl. Pour hot bacon fat vinaigrette over the salad and toss well. Adjust the seasoning with salt and pepper and serve immediately.

For the bacon fat vinaigrette

2 cloves garlic, peeled and minced
1 shallot, peeled and minced
1 tsp (5 mL) minced fresh thyme
2 Tbsp (30 mL) bacon fat
1 Tbsp (15 mL) malt vinegar
coarse salt
freshly ground black pepper

In a small saucepan over medium heat, sauté the garlic, shallot and thyme in the bacon fat, being careful not to burn anything. Deglaze the pan with the vinegar and adjust seasoning with salt and pepper. Remove and keep warm.

For the Creole yams

1 lb (500 g) sweet potatoes, peeled and diced
1 Tbsp (15 mL) sweet butter
½ cup (125 mL) brown sugar
1 orange, zest only
¼ tsp (1 mL) powdered ginger
¼ tsp (1 mL) ground nutmeg
2 cloves
freshly ground white pepper

In a large saucepan over medium heat, sauté the sweet potatoes in the butter until golden brown, about 8 minutes. Add the remaining ingredients and 1 cup (250 mL) of water and bring to a boil. Reduce the heat and cook until dry, about 20 minutes. Remove from the heat and keep warm until needed.

When ready to serve

Mound equal amounts of the Creole yams and creamed corn in the center of 4 warm dinner plates. On a clean work surface cut the quails in half and place 2 halves on the vegetables. Heat the coffee barbecue sauce and drizzle overtop. Serve the frisée salad on the side.

strip steak

one-bite Caesar | smoky rub | clam vinaigrette

In the summertime, there's nothing I like more than a steak with Caesar salad. This one comes with a twist, of course.

To build the dish
strip steaks
Caesar salad
Parmesan tuile
clam vinaigrette

Serves 4

For the strip steaks

four 12-oz (400-g) New York strip steaks
2 Tbsp (30 mL) smoky rub (recipe page 126)
1 tsp (15 mL) coarse salt
1 tsp (15 mL) olive oil
2 Tbsp (30 mL) sweet butter

Preheat oven to 350°F (180°C). Place a wire rack on a sheet pan.

Place the steaks on a clean, flat work surface and sprinkle with the smoky rub and coarse salt. Drizzle with the olive oil then use your hands to evenly coat the steaks. In a large cast iron frying pan over medium heat, sear the steaks for 3 minutes on each side. Transfer to the prepared sheet pan and roast for 5–7 minutes for medium rare. Remove from the heat and rest in a warm place until needed.

For the Caesar salad

2 egg yolks
2 fillets white anchovies
2 cloves garlic, peeled and minced
1 tsp (5 mL) capers
¼ cup (60 mL) red wine vinegar
1 lemon, juice only
1 cup (250 mL) canola oil, very cold
½ tsp (2 mL) freshly ground white pepper
5–6 heads baby romaine lettuce

In a food processor fitted with a metal blade, pulse the yolks, anchovies, garlic, capers, vinegar and lemon juice until evenly incorporated. With the food processor running very slowly, add the chilled canola oil in a thin but steady stream. The dressing should be the consistency of thick mayonnaise. Remove from the food processor, season with white pepper and transfer to a nonreactive container. Refrigerate until needed.

For the Parmesan tuile

1 cup (250 mL) freshly ground Parmesan
1 tsp (5 mL) all-purpose flour

Preheat oven to 350°F (180°C). Line a sheet pan with a non-stick silicone liner.

In a large bowl gently toss the Parmesan cheese with the flour, just enough to coat the cheese. Sprinkle the cheese mixture in 4 circles about 6 inches (15 cm) in diameter, leaving enough space for the cheese to spread. Bake on the middle rack in the oven until the cheese is light golden brown, about 4–5 minutes. Remove from the oven and using an offset spatula, carefully and quickly drape the hot cheese over a rolling pin. Allow the cheese to cool and harden into the shape from the rolling pin. Remove and store uncovered until needed.

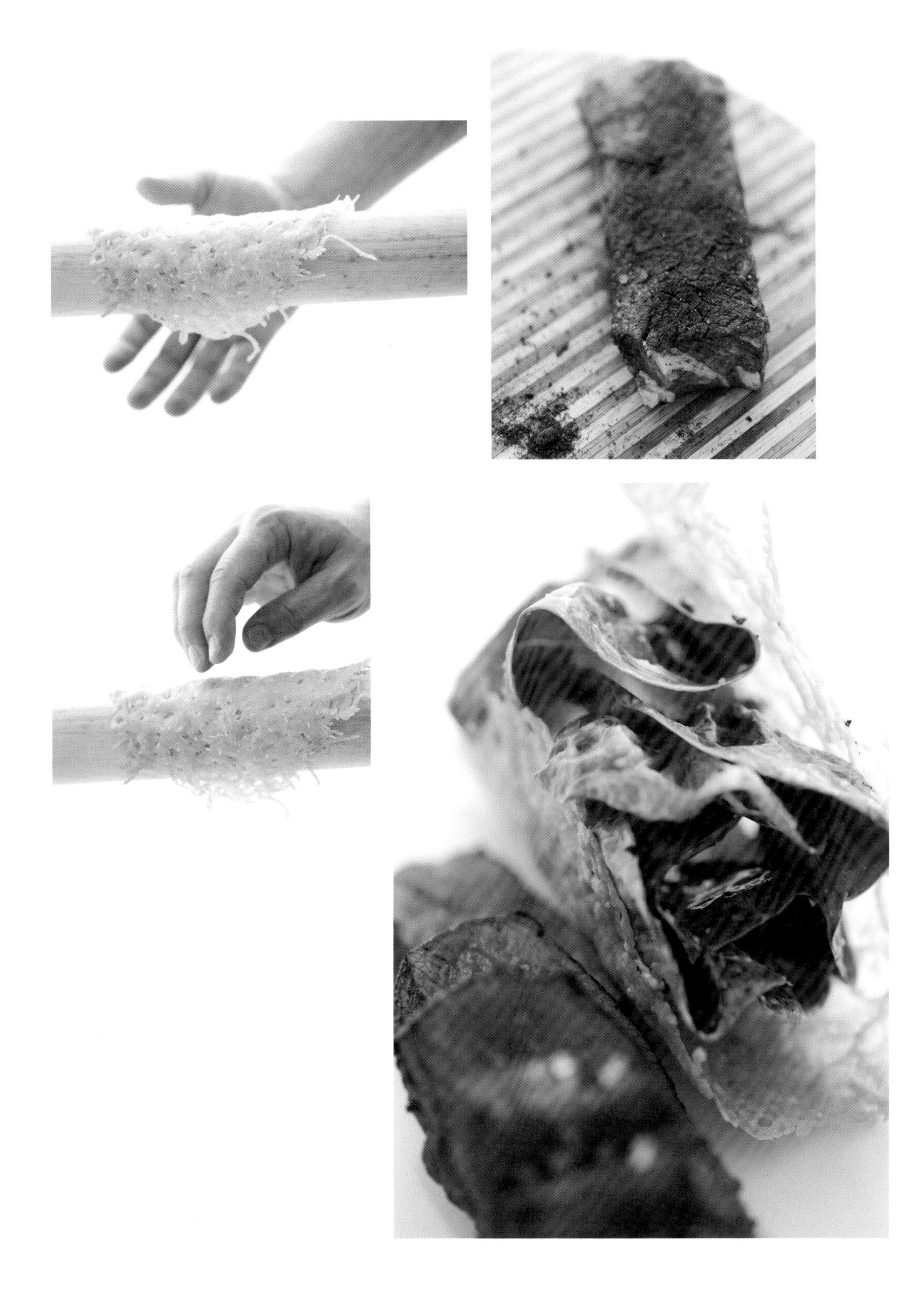

strip steak (continued)

For the clam vinaigrette

1 Tbsp (15 mL) vegetable oil
2 lb (1 kg) Manila clams
½ cup (125 mL) white wine
1 bay leaf
2 sprigs thyme
4 cloves garlic
4–5 sprigs parsley
1 small yellow pepper, roasted, peeled and seeds removed
2 scallions, washed and roots discarded
1 lemon, zest only
2 Tbsp (30 mL) sherry vinegar
½ cup (125 mL) extra virgin olive oil
freshly ground black pepper

Line a sheet pan with parchment paper.

In a large saucepan, heat the olive oil over high heat. Add the clams and sauté for 45 seconds. Carefully deglaze with the white wine and add the bay leaf, thyme, garlic and parsley. Cover and cook until most of the clams have opened. Remove from the heat and discard any unopened clams. Pour out onto the prepared sheet pan. Remove the meat and reserve, discarding the shells. Place the clam meat in a large nonreactive bowl. Cut the yellow pepper into strips about ¼-inch (0.5-cm) wide, turn and cut into ¼- x ¼-inch (0.5- x 0.5-cm) dice then add to the clams. Cut the scallions into ¼-inch (0.5-cm) segments and add to the mixture. Add the lemon zest, sherry vinegar and olive oil and gently mix until evenly distributed. Season to taste with pepper. Refrigerate, covered, until needed.

When ready to serve

On a clean work surface carve the strip steaks into ½-inch (1-cm) slices and place in the center of 4 warm dinner plates. In a large nonreactive bowl toss the baby romaine leaves with the creamy garlic dressing, divide into the Parmesan tuiles and rest against the sliced strip steak. Garnish with clam vinaigrette.

Stock for all Seasons

beef stock

5 lb (2.2 kg) beef bones
12 cups (3 L) cold water
2 carrots, peeled and chopped
2 leeks, washed and chopped
4 ribs celery, peeled and chopped
2 sprigs thyme
4 sprigs parsley
2 bay leaves
1 tsp (5 mL) black peppercorns

Rinse the bones in cold water to remove any debris. Remove and transfer to a large stockpot over low heat and bring to a simmer. Add the remaining ingredients and simmer for 2–3 hours. Remove from heat, strain and cool completely. Store covered in the refrigerator.

court bouillon

8 cups (2 L) cold water
1 cup (250 mL) white wine vinegar
1 Tbsp (15 mL) coarse salt
3 large carrots, peeled and sliced
2 onions, peeled and sliced
1 sprig thyme
3 sprigs parsley
2 bay leaves
1 tsp (5 mL) black peppercorns, crushed

In a large stockpot over medium heat add all the ingredients and bring to a simmer. Cook for 45 minutes. Remove from heat, strain and cool completely. Store covered in the refrigerator.

dark chicken stock

4 lb (1.8 kg) chicken bones
1 Tbsp (15 mL) corn oil
8 cups (2 L) cold water
2 carrots, peeled and chopped
2 leeks, washed and chopped
4 ribs celery, chopped
2 tomatoes, chopped
1 sprig thyme
2 sprigs parsley
1 bay leaf
1 tsp (5 mL) black peppercorns

Preheat oven to 325°F (160°C).

In a heavy gauge roasting pan add the bones and oil. Transfer to the bottom rack and roast until golden brown, about 30 minutes. Remove from oven and transfer to a large stockpot. Add remaining ingredients and bring to a simmer over low heat. Cook for 4–5 hours. Remove from heat, strain and cool completely. Store covered in the refrigerator.

dark roux

- 1 cup (250 mL) corn oil
- 1 cup (250 mL) all-purpose flour

In a heavy gauge skillet over high heat bring the oil to almost smoking. Gradually add the flour in thirds and stir constantly with a long handled wooden spoon. As soon as the roux has reached a dark brown color remove from heat and continue to stir until cool, about 5 minutes. Cool completely and store covered at room temperature.

duck stock

- 4 lb (1.8 kg) duck bones
- 1 Tbsp (15 mL) corn oil
- 8 cups (2 L) cold water
- 2 carrots, peeled and chopped
- 2 leeks, washed and chopped
- 4 ribs celery, chopped
- 2 tomatoes, chopped
- 1 sprig thyme
- 2 sprigs parsley
- 1 bay leaf
- 1 tsp (5 mL) black peppercorns
- 4–5 juniper berries
- 2 cloves

Preheat oven to 325°F (160°C).

In a heavy gauge roasting pan add the bones and oil. Transfer to the bottom rack and roast until golden brown, about 30 minutes. Remove from oven and transfer to a large stockpot. Add remaining ingredients and bring to a simmer over low heat. Cook for 4–5 hours. Remove from heat, strain and cool completely. Store covered in the refrigerator.

shellfish stock

- 1 lb (500 g) shells (shrimp, lobster or crab)
- 1 Tbsp (15 mL) corn oil
- 1 leek, washed and chopped
- 2 ribs celery, chopped
- 1 large carrot, peeled and chopped
- 1 Tbsp (15 mL) tomato paste
- 2 bay leaves
- 1 tsp (5 mL) black peppercorns, crushed
- ¼ cup (60 mL) vermouth
- 8 cups (2 L) cold water

In a large stockpot over medium heat sauté the shells in oil for 3–5 minutes. Add the leek, celery and carrot and continue to cook 3 minutes. Add the tomato paste and spices and cook until vegetables are well coated, about 3 minutes. Add the vermouth and water. Bring to a simmer and cook for 20 minutes. Remove from heat, strain and cool completely. Store covered in the refrigerator.

Stock for all Seasons (continued)

veal demi-glace

- 4 cups (1 L) veal jus (recipe below)
- 2 cups (500 mL) red wine

In a large stockpot over low heat reduce the veal jus and red wine until very thick and syrupy. Remove from heat, strain and cool completely. Store covered in the refrigerator.

veal jus

- 5 lb (2.2 kg) veal bones
- 1 Tbsp (15 mL) corn oil
- 12 cups (4 L) cold water
- 2 cups (500 mL) red wine
- 2 large carrots, peeled and chopped
- 2 leeks, washed and chopped
- 4 ribs celery, chopped
- ¼ cup (60 mL) tomato paste
- 2 sprigs thyme
- 4 sprigs parsley
- 2 bay leaves
- 1 tsp (5 mL) black peppercorns
- 1 tsp (5 mL) coarse salt

Preheat oven to 325°F (160°C).

Rinse the bones in cold water to remove any debris.

Transfer the bones to a large roasting pan. Drizzle with oil and roast until in oven until golden brown, about 45 minutes. Remove roasting pan from oven and place on stove. Add the remaining ingredients except water and scrape pan to dislodge the caramelization, approximately 20 minutes making sure the tomato paste is dry but not burnt. Remove from heat and transfer to the stockpot. Add water and bring to a simmer. Cook 4–5 hours. Remove from heat, strain and cool completely. Store covered in refrigerator.

vegetable stock

- 1 onion, peeled and sliced
- 1 leek, washed and chopped
- 2 ribs celery, chopped
- 1 large carrot, peeled and chopped
- 1 tsp (5 mL) corn oil
- 2 tomatoes, chopped
- 2 cloves garlic, peeled and chopped
- 8 cups (2 L) cold water
- 2 bay leaves
- 1 tsp (5 mL) black peppercorns, cracked

In a large stockpot over medium heat sweat the onion, leek, celery and carrot in oil for 5 minutes. Add the tomatoes and garlic and continue to cook 3 minutes. Add the water and spices. Bring to a simmer and continue to cook for 40 minutes. Remove from heat, strain and cool completely. Store covered in the refrigerator.

white fish rub

- 1 Tbsp (15 mL) white peppercorns
- 1 Tbsp (15 mL) coriander seeds
- 1 tsp (5 mL) chili flakes
- 1 tsp (5 mL) fennel seeds
- 1 tsp (5 mL) ground nutmeg

Combine all ingredients in a spice grinder and blend until fine, about 20 seconds. Remove and store in sealed container.

white fish stock

- 1 Tbsp (15 mL) corn oil
- 3 lb (1.5 kg) fish bones (halibut, flounder or sole)
- 2 large carrots, peeled and chopped
- 2 ribs celery, chopped
- 1 leek, washed and chopped
- 8 cups (2 L) cold water
- 1 cup (250 mL) white wine
- 3 sprigs parsley
- 2 sprigs tarragon
- 1 bay leaf
- 1 tsp (5 mL) black peppercorns, crushed

In a large stockpot over medium heat sweat the bones, carrots, celery and leek in oil for 4–5 minutes. Add the remaining ingredients and bring to a simmer. Cook for 30 minutes. Remove from heat, strain and cool completely. Store covered in the refrigerator.

black olive spread

- 1 cup (250 mL) sun-dried black olives
- ¼ cup (60 mL) extra virgin olive oil
- coarse salt
- freshly ground black pepper

On a clean work surface press the olives to expose the pits. Discard pits and transfer to a food processor fitted with a metal blade and purée. Slowly add the olive oil and continue to blend until smooth. Season with salt and pepper. Remove and store covered in the refrigerator.

sun-dried tomato spread

- 1 cup (250 mL) sun-dried tomatoes
- 2 Tbsp (30 mL) olive oil
- 1 shallot, peeled and sliced
- 2 cloves garlic, peeled and sliced
- 1 Tbsp (15 mL) smoked paprika
- coarse salt
- freshly ground black pepper

Soak sun-dried tomatoes in warm water to soften, about 20 minutes. Drain and reserve. In a saucepan over medium heat sweat the shallots and garlic in olive oil until translucent, about 3–4 minutes. Remove from the heat and transfer to a food processor fitted with a metal blade. Add the sun-dried tomatoes and paprika and blend until smooth. Season with salt and pepper. Remove and store covered in the refrigerator.

vegetable shred

- 1 red pepper, julienne
- 1 yellow pepper, julienne
- 1 large carrot, peeled and julienne
- 4 scallions, julienne

Combine all ingredients in a large bowl of ice water and let soak for 10 minutes. Remove, drain and store covered in the refrigerator.

Glossary

achiote paste
Seeds of the annatto tree are ground down to make achiote paste. The paste has an earthy taste, with a hint of iodine. It is most commonly used as a coloring agent—it is used commercially to color cheddar cheeses and butter—and is good when used in slow-cooked sauces and stews.

acini de pepe pasta
Italian for "peppercorns," this pasta looks like tiny beads. It expands considerably when cooked.

acorn squash
Acorn squash (Cucurbita pepo) is a dark green, winter squash with sweet, yellow-orange flesh.

allspice berries
More accurately, this is a single berry from the Jamaican bayberry tree. It has a heavy sweetness, which gives allspice its versatility. It tastes similar to cloves, cinnamon and nutmeg. The whole berries are used in poached fish stock, vegetable and fruit pickles and for wild game. The ground berries can be used in spice cakes, puddings and other desserts. Allspice is a great secret ingredient when making your own barbecue sauce. It's also a key ingredient in Caribbean jerk dishes.

Angostura Bitters
These aromatic bitters are made in Trinidad; orange peel and gentian are its main ingredients. Gentian is a moderately tall perennial herb with an erect stem and large ovate leaves with large orange and yellow flowers.

annatto seed
Also known as achiote seed, this is used as a coloring agent in butter, margarine, cheese and smoked fish.(See also achiote paste.)

aspiration
A hybrid of the cabbage family, this cross between broccoli and Chinese kale is also known as broccolini.

banana leaf
Banana leaves are often used as a decorative serving vessel or aromatic wrapper, and are a key decorative element in some Hindu and Buddhist ceremonies. They are also sometimes used to prepare fish for baking, and are the perfect answer when you're looking for a beautiful, biodegradable wrapper to serve single-serving rice dishes.

biryani
This is an Indian dish containing meat, fish, or vegetables and rice, which is flavored with saffron or turmeric.

blackstrap molasses
Molasses is a thick dark syrup that is a byproduct of sugar refining. Blackstrap molasses comes from the third boiling of the sugar cane and is basically the dregs of the barrel, making it extra dark, very thick and somewhat bitter. It's nothing if not versatile, being used in the manufacturing of alcohol and as an ingredient to cattle feed, as well as for baking and sauces.

buttermilk
Despite its name, buttermilk contains no butter. It's actually composed of skim milk and bacterial cultures and is produced in a similar way to yogurt and sour cream. It is most often used in baked goods to give a rich, tangy flavor and is perfect for deep-fried onion ring batter.

chervil
Chervil, also known as French parsley, has a delicate licorice flavor with the mild pepperiness of parsley. Its subtle fleeting flavor is destroyed by cooking and drying, so use large quantities of fresh leaves toward the end of cooking.

chicory
This curly endive lettuce, called frisée by the French, has a bitter aftertaste. It is often used as a great side addition with rich and heavy dishes, such as pork, to cut through the flavor. The roots of this herb are dried, ground, roasted and used to flavor coffee.

chiffonade
This refers to a small chopped pile of thin strips of an ingredient. Usually it is raw, but sometimes sautéed. Mostly used for garnish, the literal translation from French means "made from rags."

Chinese cabbage
Also known as Napa cabbage, celery cabbage and bok choy, Chinese cabbage has elongated leaves and very distinctive crinkled leaves. Often used in Asian cuisine for its tender flavor and more appealing style, it's also used to wrap proteins such as duck or a vegetable combination.

cipolline
Pronounced *chip-oh-LEE-nee,* these are small, flat, pale onions, making them ideal for roasting. They're sweeter than garden-variety white or yellow onions as they have more residual sugar. They are harvested in the fall and may not be easily available year round.

clarified butter

Also called drawn butter, clarified butter is made clear by heating and removing the milk solids sediment. This also gives clarified butter a higher smoke point than regular butter and it may therefore be used for cooking at higher temperatures. It also has a longer shelf life than normal butter. Ghee is an East Indian form of highly clarified butter.

cloudberry jus

These berries are found in low-populated areas throughout central Canada. They are related to the raspberry but are bigger and taste like a cross between passion fruit and apricot. Cloudberry jus is often eaten as a preserve on toast or fresh bread.

collard greens

Collard greens are kale leaves used as a vegetable. They are often paired with bacon lardoons in southern-style cooking.

court bouillon

A vegetable broth made by simmering onions (or leeks), carrots, celery, and sometimes other vegetables, such as fennel, with a bouquet garni in water and often white wine or vinegar (see recipe page 148).

creole mustard

Creole mustard is made from a secret Cajun recipe that dates back to the mid-1800s. Spicy but not too hot, it can be used on just about everything and is often found in ham sandwiches.

daikon

Daikon is a large Japanese radish that can be eaten raw or cooked.

dark roux

The usual portion of fat to flour in a roux is 50:50, with the fat being oil, butter or lard. The color of the roux depends on how long it's cooked. Light- and medium-colored roux are normally used in sauces, whereas dark roux is used for gravies and dishes requiring a nuttier flavor.

deglaze

This is a method of removing browned bits of food from the bottom of a pan after sautéing. After food and excess fat have been removed from the pan, a small amount of liquid is heated with the cooking juices in the pan and stirred to remove browned bits of food—usually meat—from the bottom. The resulting mixture often becomes the base for a sauce.

elephant ear mushrooms

Also known as flower coral, resembling sea coral, the elephant ear mushroom is brown and green with a large wavy surface and leathery texture. It has an earthy moss flavor and is most commonly used in vegetarian Chinese cuisine.

epazote

Also known as Mexican tea, this is a pungent herb used in Mexican and South American cooking. Like cilantro (coriander), it can be an acquired taste. The aroma and flavor have been described as medicinal or turpentine or camphor-like. Widely used in bean dishes, it is supposed to reduce the after-effects of eating beans.

escabèche

Originating from Spain, escabèche (known as escovitch in Jamaica) is poached or fried fish marinated in an acidic mixture for at least 24 hours before serving. Popular in Spain and the Provence region of France, it is usually served cold as an appetizer.

fish sauce

This condiment is made from fermented anchovies, salt and water and is common in Cambodian, Vietnamese and Thai cooking. The Cambodian version, nam pla, is considered the finest, and has the richest flavor. The Vietnamese variety, nuoc mam, which is also the most widely available, is milder. The different varieties are interchangeable according to taste. It can be found in Asian markets and some general supermarkets.

foie gras

Literally goose liver in French, foie gras is the grossly enlarged liver from duck or geese (classically from the moulard duck). The Egyptians are said to have discovered this rich delicacy, when they realized the birds store their fat before migration.

fronds

Frond refers to the leaf structure of ferns. It is used to refer to the leaves of palms, cycads and other plants with feather-like leaves.

grape leaves

Grape leaves are commonly found in Greek cooking and are often used to wrap a combination of rice fillings. They are picked fresh and blanched quickly in hot water then cooled and used as a wrap. You can purchase prepared grape leaves packaged in jars in any grocery store. The leaves have a small bitter flavor with a slightly astringent aftertaste.

Glossary (continued)

grape seed oil
From the seeds of grapes, this oil contains more linoleic acid than many other oils. Because of its neutral taste, grape seed oil is often used as an ingredient in salad dressings or as a base for infusing or flavoring with garlic, rosemary or other herbs or spices. It can also be used in homemade mayonnaise.

grits
Grits are corn kernels that are dried, hulled and finely ground then boiled and served for breakfast or as a side dish with dinner.

gumbo
This Creole specialty is a mainstay of New Orleans cuisine. It's a thick, stew-like dish that can contain any of many ingredients, including vegetables such as okra, tomatoes and onions, and one or several meats or shellfish such as chicken, sausage, ham, shrimp, crab or oysters. The one thing with which all good gumbos begin is a dark roux, which adds an unmistakable, incomparably rich flavor.

haricots verts
The French equivalent of green string beans, they tend to be more delicate in size and flavor than their anglophone rivals and are the preference of chefs around the world.

heart of palm
The edible inner portion of the stem of the cabbage palm tree, which grows in many tropical climates, resembles white asparagus. Normally used in salads (called "millionaire's salad") hearts of palm are only available fresh in areas where they are grown, such as Florida. You can find them canned in any supermarket.

hominy
This term refers to corn without the germ. It is served both whole and ground and can be boiled until cooked and served as either a cereal or as a vegetable. Hominy may also be pressed into patties and fried and is available in cans.

jicama
Pronounced *HE-ke-ma*, jicama is also known as the "Mexican potato, yam bean and turnip." It's grown for its large tuberous roots which can be eaten raw or cooked and are used as a source of starch.

kaffir lime leaves
The kaffir lime, also known as kieffer lime, makrut or magrood, is a Southeast Asian citrus plant with very pungent, hourglass-shaped leaves and a bumpy exterior. The leaves are widely used in Thai and Lao cuisine.

Korean kochujang
This Korean red pepper paste is very spicy and commonly used in Korean rice dishes to impart some traditional flavoring.

lemon grass
Lemon grass, or lemongrass, is a perennial herb used in Asian (particularly Thai, Lao, Khmer and Vietnamese) and Caribbean cooking. It has a lemony flavor and can be dried and powdered, or used fresh. It's commonly used in teas, soups and curries, and is also suitable for poultry, fish and seafood.

mandoline (Japanese)
The Japanese version of the mandoline is the less expensive, but equally versatile and effective, option for slicing, julienning and fine dicing. This is the sharpest tool in any kitchen and must be treated with caution and respect. It's mainly used for vegetables to give them volume when sliced for a more appealing look to a dish.

Manila clams
Manilas are considered to be very tender and sweet. Originating from Japan, they are gathered by hand rake. In British Columbia, Canada, Manila clams are cultured and collected from wild beds but today, most production comes from Washington State.

masa harina
This flour-like powder is made with sun- or fire-dried corn kernels that have been cooked in limewater (water mixed with calcium oxide). After having been cooked and soaked in the limewater overnight, the wet corn is ground into masa harina. Often used in Mexican cooking, it can be found in any Latino market.

Mexican chocolate
This chocolate is flavored with cinnamon, almonds and vanilla. It is available in Mexican markets and is used for hot chocolate or mole sauces.

mirin
Sweetened sake (Japanese rice wine).

mole
Any of the various spicy sauces of Mexican origin, which usually have a base of onion, chilies, nuts or seeds, and unsweetened chocolate (Mexican chocolate) and is served with meat or poultry. Dry versions can be commonly found jarred and canned.

monkfish
Monkfish is also known as angel shark. With broad flat bodies and wing-like pectoral fins, they swim like sharks and can easily be distinguished by their large heads, wide mouths and ugly appearance. The tail meat is widely used and is often compared to lobster.

Old Bay seasoning
Old Bay seasoning is a blend of herbs and spices currently marketed by McCormick & Company. It's named for the Chesapeake Bay area where it was invented in the 1940s by a German immigrant named Gustav Brunn. The seasoning mix includes celery, bay leaf, mustard seed, red pepper and ginger and is traditionally used in New England to season crab and shrimp.

Panko breadcrumbs
American breadcrumbs originated around 1947; Panko breadcrumbs originated in Japan around 1970. There are many differences between the two crumb styles, with the main ones being the texture and density. American crumbs are heavier and denser than the Japanese crumbs.

parsley root
Also called Hamburg parsley and turnip-rooted parsley, this parsley subspecies is grown for its beige, carrot-like root, which tastes like a carrot-celery cross. It's used in parts of Europe in soups, stews and simply as a vegetable. Choose firm roots with feathery, bright-green leaves. Refrigerate in a plastic bag for up to a week.

pink peppercorns
Pink peppercorns are from Brazil but are not a true peppercorn. They are actually the dried fruit of the baies roses. The berries have a sweet peppery flavor and are quite popular in French cuisine. Use them in vinaigrettes or crush them to use as a coating for a filet mignon or pork tenderloin.

piquillo peppers
Piquillo is the Spanish word for little beak, which is the shape of the pepper. These peppers are grown in northern Spain and are hand picked, roasted over an open fire, peeled and packed in their own juices. Roasting the peppers enhances their rich piquant flavor.

plantains
Green plantains, which are very hard and starchy with little banana flavor and no sweetness, are generally cooked in the same ways as potatoes. They can be boiled or fried or added to soups and stews. Yellow-ripe plantains, which are more tender, can be used in these same ways but will have a creamier texture. They can also be mashed, grilled or baked.

plantain chips
Plantains belong to the banana family but are longer than bananas and have thicker skin. They can be eaten as a casual snack and are a decorative element in plating a dish. They are used for chips when the plantain is green (unripe) so they tend to taste starchy like a potato. If the chips are made of sweeter ripened fruit, they are called banana chips.

poblano pepper
The poblano is a mild chili pepper that can be dried, breaded and fried, stuffed, or used in sauces called moles. It is a dark, sometimes almost black green pepper, and is known for its use in chili relannos.

pomegranate
Native from Iran to the Himalayas, pomegranate was introduced to California by Spanish settlers. The sack-filled fruit is protected by a thick, leathery red skin, and its interior is protected by a membrane that helps to compartmentalize dozens of fruit juice-filled sacks, each containing a seed. Pomegranate juice is very sweet and acidic and has recently been described as an antioxidant.

pomegranate molasses
This stunning, deep ruby-colored syrup is both sweet and sour. It lends itself beautifully to being drizzled on soups, grains, and used as a base for drinks. This molasses gives a tannic touch to cooking flavour.

poussin
A poussin is a small immature chicken, also called a spring chicken.

Glossary (continued)

purple potatoes
Purple potatoes are small, oval-shaped potatoes with a purplish-black outer skin and vivid purple, dense inner meat.

russet potatoes
Also known as Burbank potatoes, these are oblong in shape with brown skin and a white interior.

Savoy cabbage
This mellow-flavored cabbage is considered by many to be one of the best of its genre for cooking. Savoy has a loose, full head of crinkled leaves varying in color from dark to pale green. Choose a head that's heavy for its size. The leaves should be crisp, not limp, and there should be no sign of browning.

sea beans
Also known as sea asparagus, sea beans belong to the genus *Salicornia,* making them a distant relative of beets and spinach. Sea beans are an intertidal plant, which means it grows in brackish water near the edge of the ocean. They are high in salt and so you should exercise caution when seasoning any dish containing sea beans.

semolina flour
Semolina flour is ground from hard durum winter wheat. It produces stronger dough because it contains a high level of gluten, which adds elasticity. Dough made from semolina flour is easier to form into different shapes and can be sent through an electric pasta machine but it's too difficult to handle when rolling out by hand because of its stickiness. Semolina flour can be mixed with unbleached white flour to produce strong dough that is easier to handle when making handmade pasta.

skate wing
Skates are cartilaginous fish belonging to the ray-fish family. Only their wings are eaten, and they are a delicacy mainly in Europe, particularly when fried in butter. Even though many people think they haven't eaten skate wings before, many unscrupulous fish markets have been found to counterfeit sea scallops out of skate wings because of their similar texture and flavors.

smoked paprika
Spanish smoked paprika comes dolce (sweet), agridulce (semisweet) or picante (hot). Look for brands that come from La Vera where the climate and the process of smoke-drying produce the quality Spanish paprika. This precious powder is indispensable for Spanish dishes. It adds the absolutely perfect taste of authenticity to paellas.

snow pea tendrils
These are the vines upon which snow peas grow and are most commonly used in salads and stir-fry. They are harvested young, before they bear fruit, which keeps them tender.

spaetzle
Originating from Germany, these small dumplings are popular in the Alto Adige region of Italy. They can be made with many different ingredients, and are often served in a meat broth.

squab
Young commercially raised pigeons.

star anise
Star anise is a star-shaped dry seed pod with a flavor similar to that of fennel. It comes from China and is a member of the magnolia tree family. Like anise, it derives its distinctive flavor from anethol, but star anise is slightly more bitter. It's widely used in various Asian cuisines.

suribachi
A suribachi is a Japanese mortar and pestle made of ceramic with a wooden stick. It is most often used to grind spices, seeds and nuts.

Szechuan peppercorns
Though not related to the peppercorn family, Szechuan berries resemble black peppercorns and contain a tiny seed. They are native to the Szechuan province of China and come from the prickly ash tree. Szechuan pepper, also known as anise pepper or flower pepper, has a distinctive flavor and fragrance. It can be found in Asian markets and specialty stores in whole or powdered form. The whole berries are often heated before being ground to bring out their tantalizing flavor and aroma.

tandoori marinade
Available in Indian markets, this coloring is used to give foods the traditional red-orange tint, which is a result of tandoor oven cooking. Tandoori paste can be rubbed directly onto the surface of meats; tandoori powder is generally stirred into a marinade.

tasso ham
This lean and highly seasoned ham is served in the southern United States and is most often associated with Cajun cuisine. Sometimes referred to as Cajun ham, it has a heavily smoked, peppery outer skin. Andouille, chorizo or linguica sausage can be used as substitutes for more spicy intensity, but none of the three will provide the depth of the smoky flavor provided by tasso.

Thai bird chilies
The hottest form of chili pepper, rating a 100,000 on the Scoville pungency scale, has peppers that point downward and go directly from green to red. Also called bird's eye chili and bird pepper, it can be used both fresh and dried. The name derives from the belief that the peppers were harvested originally by birds.

traverse radicchio
Raddichio is a tender but firm variety of chicory with a slightly bitter taste. It has small hearts, is red with white veins and is generally used in mixed salads.

Tuscan bread
To this day, the bread served in Florence and throughout Tuscany is unlike that of other regions. The large, thick-crusted oval loaves are made without salt. Flat bread, schiacciata rusks, focaccia and breadsticks are also salt-free.

veal jus
This is a most versatile stock used for soups and sauces (see recipe page 150).

veal demi-glace
Also known as glace de viande, this is simply veal stock that is slowly reduced to a syrupy consistency (see recipe page 150). It is the foundation of most meat sauces. Although the process for making veal demi-glace is lengthy, it is neither laborious nor does it take any special skill. It is also available in quality supermarkets.

veal rib eye
Rib eye comes from the same muscle that gives us those exquisite top loin and top sirloin cuts. This cut can be roasted to make a boneless version of a rib roast, or cut into individual steaks, called rib eye steaks. Rib eye roasts are very tender, well marbled with fat and fairly expensive.

white asparagus
White asparagus is the variety referred in Europe. The sunlight-deprived stalks are a little milder and more delicate than the purple and green varieties.

white cornmeal
Cornmeal can be yellow, white or blue, depending on the type of corn used. Yellow cornmeal contains slightly more vitamin A than white cornmeal.

white snow fungus
Snow fungus is a type of mushroom or jelly fungus and is native to Japan. It is purchased dried and must be soaked before using. It's normally added to dishes for its interesting texture as its flavor is neutral. It's also used in Chinese medicine for its healing properties, particularly for lung-related conditions.

white vinegar
White vinegar is a clear liquid used in all forms of culinary cooking and is most often used in salad dressings. It's made from grain (often maize) and water and then oxidized as a distilled alcohol. Most commercial white vinegars are 5 percent acetic acid solutions.

wild rice
Wild rice is the seed of a plume-topped wild aquatic grass found mainly in the northern central United States and Canada. It is expensive due to short supply and the cost of hand gathering and thrashing, and is often mixed with other types of rice or grain.

Index